John S. Blackie

Self-Culture, Physical, Intellectual and Moral

a vade mecum for young men and students

John S. Blackie

Self-Culture, Physical, Intellectual and Moral
a vade mecum for young men and students

ISBN/EAN: 9783337882167

Printed in Europe, USA, Canada, Australia, Japan

Cover: Foto ©Lupo / pixelio.de

More available books at **www.hansebooks.com**

SELF-CULTURE

Intellectual, Physical, and Moral

A Vade Mecum for Young Men and Students

BY

JOHN STUART BLACKIE,

PROFESSOR OF GREEK IN THE UNIVERSITY OF EDINBURGH

EDINBURGH: DAVID DOUGLAS
1889

[All rights reserved.]

CONTENTS

	PAGE
THE CULTURE OF THE INTELLECT	1
ON PHYSICAL CULTURE	39
ON MORAL CULTURE	55

THE CULTURE OF THE INTELLECT.

Es ist immer gut etwas zu wissen.—GOETHE.

THE CULTURE OF THE INTELLECT.

1. IN modern times instruction is communicated chiefly by means of BOOKS. Books are no doubt very useful helps to knowledge, and in some measure also, to the practice of useful arts and accomplishments, but they are not, in any case, the primary and natural sources of culture, and, in my opinion, their virtue is not a little apt to be overrated, even in those branches of acquirement where they seem most indispensable. They are not creative powers in any sense; they are merely helps, instruments, tools; and even as tools they are only artificial tools, superadded to those with which the wise prevision of Nature has equipped us, like telescopes and microscopes, whose assistance in many researches reveals unimagined wonders, but the use of which should never tempt us to undervalue or to neglect the exercise of our own eyes. The original and proper sources of knowledge are not books, but life, experience, personal thinking, feeling, and acting. When a man starts with these, books can fill up many gaps, correct much that is in-

accurate, and extend much that is inadequate; but, without living experience to work on, books are like rain and sunshine fallen on unbroken soil.

"The parchment roll is that the holy river,
From which one draught shall slake the thirst for ever?
The quickening power of science only he
Can know, from whose own soul it gushes free."

This is expressed, no doubt, somewhat in a poetical fashion, but it contains a great general truth. As a treatise on mineralogy can convey no real scientific knowledge to a man who has never seen a mineral, so neither can works of literature and poetry instruct the mere scholar who is ignorant of life, nor discourses on music him who has no experience of sweet sounds, nor gospel sermons him who has no devotion in his soul or purity in his life. All knowledge which comes from books comes indirectly, by reflection, and by echo; true knowledge grows from a living root in the thinking soul; and whatever it may appropriate from without, it takes by living assimilation into a living organism, not by mere borrowing.

II. I therefore earnestly advise all young men to commence their studies, as much as possible, by direct OBSERVATION of FACTS, and not by the mere inculcation of statements from books. A useful book was written with the title,—*How to Observe*. These three words might serve as a motto to guide us in the most important part of our early education—a part, unfortunately, only too much neglected. All the natural sciences are particularly valuable, not only as supplying the mind with the most rich, various, and beautiful furniture, but as teaching people that most useful of all arts, how to use their eyes. It is astonishing how much we all go about with our eyes open, and yet seeing nothing. This is because the organ of vision, like other organs, requires training; and by lack of training and the slavish dependence on books, becomes dull and slow, and ultimately incapable of exercising its natural function. Let those studies, therefore, both in school and college, be regarded as primary, that teach young persons to know what they are seeing, and to see what they otherwise would fail to see. Among the most useful are, Botany, Zoology, Mineralogy, Geology, Chemistry, Architecture, Drawing, and the Fine Arts. How many a Highland excursion and continental tour have been rendered comparatively useless to young persons well drilled in their books, merely from the want of a little elementary knowledge in these sciences of observation.

III. Observation is good, and accurate observation is better; but, on account of the vast variety of objects in the universe, the observing faculty would be overwhelmed and confounded, did we not possess some sure method of submitting their multitude to a certain regulative principle placing them under the control of our minds. This regulative principle is what we call CLASSIFICATION, and is discoverable by human reason, because it clearly exists every-

where in a world which is the manifestation of
Divine reason. This classification depends on
the fundamental unity of type which the Divine
reason has imposed on all things. This unity
manifests itself in the creation of points of likeness in things apparently the most different;
and it is these points of likeness which, when
seized by a nicely observant eye, enable it to
distribute the immense variety of things in the
world into certain parcels of greater or less compass, called genera and species, which submit
themselves naturally to the control of a com-
paring and discriminating mind. The first business of the student, therefore, is, in all that he
sees, to observe carefully the points of likeness,
and, along with these, also the most striking
points of difference; for the points of difference go
as necessarily along with the points of likeness,
as shadow goes along with light; and though
they do not of themselves constitute any actual
thing, yet they separate one genus from another,
and one species of the same genus from another.
The classification or order to be sought for in
all things is a natural order; artificial arrange-
ments, such as that of words in an alphabetical
dictionary, or of flowers in the Linnæan system
of botany, may be useful helps to learners in an
early stage, but, if exclusively used, are rather
hindrances to true knowledge. What a young
man should aim at is to acquire a habit of
binding things together according to their bonds
of natural affinity; and this can be done only
by a combination of a broad view of the general
effect, with an accurate observation of the spe-

cial properties. The names given by the common people to flowers are instances of superficial similarity, without any attempt at discrimination, as when a water-lily seems by its name to indicate that it is a species of lily, with which flower it has no real connection. A botanist, on the other hand, who has minutely observed the character and organs of plants, will class a water-lily rather with the papaverous or poppy family, and give you very good reasons for doing so. In order to assist in forming habits of observation in this age of locomotion, I should advise young men never to omit visiting the local museums of any district, as often as they may have an opportunity; and when there to confine their attention generally to that one thing which is most characteristic of the locality. Looking at everything generally ends in remembering nothing.

IV. Upon the foundation of carefully-observed and well-assorted facts the mind proceeds to build a more subtle structure by the process which we call REASONING. We would know not only that things *are* so and so, but *how* they are, and *for what purpose* they are. The essential unity of the Divine Mind causes a necessary unity in the processes by which things exist and grow, no less than a unity in the type of their manifold genera and species; and into both manifestations of Divine unity we are, by the essential unity of our divinely emanated human souls, compelled to enquire. Our human reason, as proceeding from the Divine reason, is constantly employed in working out a unity, or consistency of plan, to speak more popularly, in the processes of our own little lives ; and we are thus naturally determined to seek for such a unity, consistency, and necessary dependence, in all the operations of a world which exists only, as has been well said, " in reason, by reason, and for reason."* The quality of mind, which determines a man to seek out this unity in the chain of things, is what phrenologists call causality ; for the cause of a thing, as popularly understood, is merely that point in the necessary succession of divinely-originated forces which immediately precedes it. There are few human beings so contentedly superficial as to feed habitually on the knowledge of mere unexplained facts ; on the contrary, as we find every day, the ready assumption of any cause for a fact, rather than remain content with none, affords ample proof that the search for causes is characteristic of every normal human intellect. What young men have chiefly to look to in this matter is to avoid being imposed on by the easy habit of taking an accidental sequence or circumstance for a real cause. It may be easy to understand that the abundant rain on the west coast of Britain is caused by the vicinity of the Atlantic Ocean ; and not very difficult to comprehend how the comparative mildness of the winter season at Oban, as compared with Edinburgh or Aberdeen, is caused by the impact of a broad current of warm

* Stirling on Protoplasm—a masterly tract.

water from the Gulf of Mexico. But in the region of morals and politics, where facts are often much more complex, and passions are generally strong, we constantly find examples of a species of reasoning which assumes without proving the causal dependency of the facts of which it is based. I once heard a political discourse by a noted demagogue, which consisted of the assertion, in various forms and with various illustrations, of the proposition that all the miseries of this country arise from its monarchico-aristocratic government, and that they could all be cured, as by the stroke of a magician's wand, by the introduction of a perfectly democratic government—a species of argumentation vitiated, as is obvious all through, by the assumption of one imaginary cause to all social evils, and an equally imaginary cure. In the cultivation of habits of correct reasoning, I would certainly, in the first place, earnestly advise young men to submit themselves for a season, after the old Platonic recipe, to a system of thorough mathematical training. This will strengthen the binding power of the mind, which is necessary for all sorts of reasoning, and teach the inexperienced really to know what necessary dependence, unavoidable sequence, or pure causality means. But they must not stop here; for the reasonings of mathematics being founded on theoretical assumptions and conditions which, when once given, are liable to no variation or disturbance, can never be an adequate discipline for the great and most important class of human conclusions, which are founded on a complexity of curiously acting and reacting facts and forces liable to various disturbing influences, which even the wisest sometimes fail to calculate correctly. On political, moral, and social questions, our reasonings are not less certain than in mathematics; they are only more difficult and more comprehensive; and the great dangers to be avoided here are one-sided observation, hasty conclusions, and the distortion of intellectual vision, caused by personal passions and party interests. The politician who fails in solving a political problem, fails not from the uncertainty of the science, but either from an imperfect knowledge of the facts, or from the action of passions and interests, which prevent him from making a just appreciation of the facts.

V. At this point I can imagine it not unlikely that some young man may be inclined to ask me whether I should advise him, with the view of strengthening his reasoning powers, to enter upon a formal study of logic and metaphysics. To this I answer, By all means, if you have first, in a natural way, as opposed to mere scholastic discipline, acquired the general habit of thinking and reasoning. A man has learned to walk first by having legs, and then by using them. After that he may go to a drill-sergeant and learn to march, and to perform various tactical evolutions, which no experience of mere untrained locomotion can produce. So exactly it is with the art of thinking. Have your thinking first, and plenty to think about, and then ask the logician to teach you to scrutinise with a nice eye the process by which you have arrived at your conclusions. In such fashion there is no doubt that the study of logic may be highly beneficial. But as this science, like mathematics, has no real contents, and merely sets forth in order the universal forms under which all thinking is exercised, it must always be a very barren affair to attempt obtaining from pure logic any rich growth of thought that will bear ripe fruit in the great garden of life. One may as well expect to make a great patriot —a Bruce or a Wallace—of a fencing master, as to make a great thinker out of a mere logician. So it is in truth with all formal studies. Grammar and rhetoric are equally barren, and bear fruit only when dealing with materials given by life and experience. A meagre soul can never be made fat, nor a narrow soul large, by studying rules of thinking. An intense vitality, a wide sympathy, a keen observation, a various experience, is worth all the logic of the schools; and yet the logic is not useless; it has a regulative, not a creative virtue; it is useful to thinking as the study of anatomy is useful to painting; it gives you a more firm hold of the jointing and articulation of your framework; but it can no more produce true knowledge than anatomy can produce beautiful painting. It performs excellent service in the exposure of error and the unveiling of sophistry; but to proceed far in the discovery of important truth, it must borrow its moving power from fountains of living water, which flow not in the schools, and its materials from the facts of the breathing universe, with which no museum is furnished. So it is likewise with metaphysics. This science is useful for two ends, first — to acquaint ourselves with the necessary limits of the human faculties; it tends to clip the wings of our conceit, and to make us feel, by a little floundering and flouncing in deep bottomless seas of speculation, that the world is a much bigger place than we had imagined, and our thoughts about it of much less significance. A negative result this, you will say, but not the less important for that; the knowledge of limits is the first postulate of wisdom, and it is better to practise walking steadily on the solid earth to which we belong, than to usurp the function of birds, like Icarus, and achieve a sorry immortality by baptizing the deep sea with our name. The other use of metaphysics is positive; it teaches us to be familiar with the great fundamental truths on which the fabric of all the sciences rests. Metaphysics is not, like logic, a purely formal science; it is, on the contrary, the science of fundamental and essential reality, of that which underlies all appearances, as the soul of a man underlies his features and his fleshly framework, and survives all changes as their permanent type. It is that which we come to when we get behind the special phenomena presented by individual sciences; it is neither botany, nor physiology, nor geology, nor astronomy, nor chemistry, nor anthropology, but those general.

all-pervading, and all-controlling powers, forces, and essences, of which each special branch of knowledge is only a single aspect or manifestation; it is the common element of all existence; and as all existence is merely a grand evolution of self-determining reason (for, were it not for the indwelling reason the world would be a chaos and not a cosmos), it follows that metaphysics is the knowledge of the absolute or cosmic reason so far as it is knowable by our limited individualised reason, and is therefore, as Aristotle long ago remarked, identical with theology.* Indeed, the idea of GOD as the absolute self-existent, self-energising, self-determining Reason, is the only idea which can make the world intelligible, and has justly been held fast by all the great thinkers of the world, from Pythagoras down to Hegel, as the alone keystone of all sane thinking. By all means, therefore, let metaphysics be studied, especially in this age and place, where the novelty of a succession of brilliant discoveries in physical science, coupled with a one-sided habit of mind, swerving with a strong bias towards what is outward and material, has led some men to imagine that in mere physics is wisdom to be found, and that the true magician's wand for striking out the most important results is induction. This is the very madness of externalism; for, on the one hand, the fundamental and most vital truths from which the possibility of all science hangs, assert

* τρία γένη τῶν θεωρητικῶν ἐπιστημῶν
Φυσικὴ, μαθηματικὴ, θεολογική. Metaph. ι. 7.

themselves before all induction; and, on the
other, the physical sciences merely describe
sequences, which the superficial may mistake for
causes. Their so-called laws are merely methods
of operation; and the operator, of whom, without transgressing their special sphere, they can
take no account, is always and everywhere the
absolute, omnipresent, all-plastic REASON, which
we call GOD, whose offspring, as the pious old
Greek poet sung, we all are, and in whom, as
the great apostle preached, we live, and move,
and have our being. An essentially reasonable
theology, and an essentially reverent speculation, are the metaphysics which a young man
may fitly commence to seek after in the schools,
but which he can find only by the experience of
a truthful and a manly life; and he will then
know that he has found it, when, like King
David and the noble army of Hebrew psalmists,
he can repose upon the quiet faith of it, like a
child upon the bosom of its mother.

VI. The next function of the mind which
requires special culture is the IMAGINATION.
I much fear neither teachers nor scholars are
sufficiently impressed with the importance of a
proper training of this faculty. Some there
may be who despise it altogether, as having to
do with fiction rather than with fact, and of no
value to the severe student who wishes to
acquire exact knowledge. But this is not the
case. It is a well-known fact that the highest
class of scientific men have been led to their
most important discoveries by the quickening

power of a suggestive imagination. Of this the poet Goethe's original observations in botany and osteology may serve as an apt witness. Imagination, therefore, is the enemy of science only when it acts without reason, that is, arbitrarily and whimsically; with reason, it is often the best and the most indispensable of allies. Besides, in history, and in the whole region of concrete facts, imagination is as necessary as in poetry; the historian, indeed, cannot invent his facts, but he must mould them and dispose them with a graceful congruity; and to do this is the work of the imagination. Fairy tales and fictitious narratives of all kinds, of course, have their value, and may be wisely used in the culture of the imagination. But by far the most useful exercise of this faculty is when it buckles itself to realities; and this I advise the student chiefly to cultivate. There is no need of going to romances for pictures of human character and fortune calculated to please the fancy and to elevate the imagination. The life of Alexander the Great, of Martin Luther, of Gustavus Adolphus, or any of those notable characters on the great stage of the world, who incarnate the history which they create, is for this purpose of more educational value than the best novel that ever was written, or even the best poetry. Not all minds delight in poetry; but all minds are impressed and elevated by an imposing and a striking fact. To exercise the imagination on the lives of great and good men brings with it a double gain; for by this exercise we learn at a single stroke, and in the most effective way, both what was done and what ought to be done. But to train the imagination adequately, it is not enough that elevating pictures be made to float pleasantly before the fancy; from such mere passiveness of mental attitude no strength can grow. The student should formally call upon his imaginative faculty to take a firm grasp of the lovely shadows as they pass, and not be content till— closing the gray record—he can make the whole storied procession pass before him in due order, with appropriate badges, attitude, and expression. As there are persons who seem to walk through life with their eyes open, seeing nothing, so there are others who read through books, and perhaps even cram themselves with facts, without carrying away any living pictures of significant story which might arouse the fancy in an hour of leisure, or gird them with endurance in a moment of difficulty. Ask yourself, therefore, always when you have read a chapter of any notable book, not what you saw printed on a gray page, but what you see pictured in the glowing gallery of your imagination. Have your fancy always vivid, and full of body and colour. Count yourself not to know a fact when you know that it took place, but then only when you see it as it did take place.

VII. The word imagination, though denoting a faculty which in some degree may be regarded as belonging to every human being, seems more particularly connected with that class of intellectual perceptions and emotions which, for want of a native term, we are accustomed to call æsthetical. A man may live, and live bravely, without much imagination, as a house may be well compacted to keep out wind and rain, and let in light, and yet be ugly. But no one would voluntarily prefer to live in an ugly house if he could get a beautiful one. So beauty, which is the natural food of a healthy imagination, should be sought after by every one who wishes to achieve the great end of existence—that is, to make the most of himself. If it is true, as we have just remarked, that man liveth not by books alone, it is equally true that he liveth not by knowledge alone. " It is always good to know something," was the wise utterance of one of the wisest men of modern times ; but by this utterance he did not mean to assert that mere indiscriminate knowing is always good ; what he meant to say was that it is wise for a man to pick up carefully, for possible uses, whatever may fall under his eye, even though it should not be the best. The best, of course, is not always at command ; and the bad, on which we frequently stumble, is not without its good element, which one should not disdain to secure in passing ; but what the young man ought to set before him, as a worthy object of systematic pursuit, is not knowledge in general, or of anything indifferently, but knowledge of what is great, and beautiful, and good ; and this, so far as the imagination is concerned, can be attained only by some special attention paid to the æsthetical culture of the intellect. In other words, poetry, painting, music, and the fine arts generally, which delight to manifest the sublime and the beautiful in every various aspect and attitude, fall under the category, not of an accidental accomplishment, but of an essential and most noble blossom of a cultivated soul. A man who knows merely with a keen glance, and acts with a firm hand, may do very well for the rough work of the world, but he may be a very ungracious and unlovely creature withal; angular, square, dogmatical, persistent, pertinacious, pugnacious, blushless, and perhaps bumptious. To bevel down the corners of a character so constituted by a little æsthetical culture, were a work of no small benefit to society, and a source of considerable comfort to the creature himself. Let a young man, therefore, commence with supplying his imaginative faculty with its natural food in the shape of beautiful objects of every kind. If there is a fine building recently erected in the town, let him stand and look at it; if there are fine pictures exhibited, let him never be so preoccupied with the avocations of his own special business that he cannot afford even a passing glance to steal a taste of their beauty; if there are dexterous riders and expert tumblers in the circus, let him not imagine that their supple somersets are mere idle tricks to amuse children: they are cunning exhibitions of the wonderful strength and litheness of the human limbs, which every wise man ought to admire. In general, let the young man, ambitious of intellectual excellence, cultivate admiration; it is by admiration only of what is beautiful and sublime that we can mount up a few steps towards the likeness of what we admire; and he who wonders not largely and habitually, in the midst of this magnificent universe, does not prove that the world has nothing great in it worthy of wonder, but only that his own sympathies are narrow, and his capacities small. The worst thing a young man can do, who wishes to educate himself æsthetically, according to the norm of nature, is to begin criticising, and cultivating the barren graces of the NIL ADMIRARI. This maxim may be excusable in a worn-out old cynic, but is intolerable in the mouth of a hopeful young man. There is no good to be looked for from a youth who, having done no substantial work of his own, sets up a business of finding faults in other people's work, and calls this practice of finding fault criticism. The first lesson that a young man has to learn, is not to find fault, but to perceive beauties. All criticism worthy of the name is the ripe fruit of combined intellectual insight and long experience. Only an old soldier can tell how battles ought to be fought. Young men of course may and ought to have opinions on many subjects, but there is no reason why they should print them. The published opinions of persons whose judgment has not been matured by experience can tend only to mislead the public, and to debauch the mind of the writer.

 I have said that the sublime and the beautiful in nature and art are the natural and healthy food of the æsthetical faculties. The comical and humorous are useful only in a subsidiary way. It is a great loss to a man when he cannot laugh; but a smile is useful specially in enabling us lightly to shake off the incongruous, not in teaching us to cherish it. Life is an earnest business, and no man was ever made great or good by a diet of broad grins. The grandest humour, such as that of Aristophanes, is valuable only as the seasoning of the pudding or the spice of the pie. No one feeds on mere pepper or vanilla. Let a young man furnish his soul richly, like Thorwaldsen's Museum at Copenhagen, with all shapes and forms of excellence, from the mild dignity of our Lord and the Twelve Apostles to the playful grace of Grecian Cupids and Hippocampes; but let him not deal in mere laughter, or corrupt his mind's eye with the habitual contemplation of distortion and caricature. There is no more sure sign of a shallow mind than the habit of seeing always the ludicrous side of things; for the ludicrous, as Aristotle remarks, is always on the surface. If the humorous novels and sketches of character in which this country and this age are so fruitful, are taken only as an occasional recreation, like a good comedy, they are to be commended; but the practice and study of the Fine Arts offer a more healthy variety to severe students than the converse with ridiculous sketches of a trifling or contemptible humanity; and to play a pleasant tune on the piano, or turn a wise saying of some ancient sage into the terms of a terse English couplet, will always be a more profitable way of unbending from the stern work of pure science, than the reading of what are called amusing books — an occupation fitted specially for the most stagnant moments of life, and the most lazy-minded of the living.

VIII. The next faculty of the mind that demands special culture is MEMORY. It is of no use gathering treasures if we cannot store them ; it is equally useless to learn what we cannot retain in the memory. Happily, of all mental faculties this is that one which is most certainly improved by exercise; besides there are helps to a weak memory such as do not exist for a weak imagination or a weak reasoning power. The most important points to be attended to in securing the retention of facts once impressed on the imagination, are—(1) The distinctness, vividness, and intensity of the original impression. Let no man hope to remember what he only vaguely and indistinctly apprehends. A multitude of dim and weak impressions, flowing in upon the mind in a hurried way, soon vanish in a haze, which veils all things, and shows nothing. It is better for the memory to have a distinct idea of one fact of a great subject, than to have confused ideas of the whole. (2) Nothing helps the memory so much as order and classification. Classes are always few, individuals many ; to know the class well is to know what is most essential in the character of the individual, and what least burdens the memory to retain. (3) The next important matter is repetition : if the nail will

not go in at one stroke, let it have another and
another. In this domain nothing is denied to
a dogged pertinacity. A man who finds it
difficult to remember that DEVA is the Sanscrit
for a GOD, has only to repeat it seven times a
day, or seven times a week, and he will not
forget it. The less tenacious a man's memory
naturally is, the more determined ought he to
be to complement it by frequent inculcation.
Our faculties, like a slow beast, require flogging
occasionally, or they make no way. (4) Again,
if memory be weak, causality is perhaps strong;
and this point of strength, if wisely used, may
readily be made to turn an apparent loss into a
real gain. Persons of very quick memory may
be apt to rest content with the faculty, and
exhibit with much applause the dexterity only
of an intellectual parrot ; but the man who is
slow to remember without a reason, searches
after the causal connection of the facts, and,
when he has found it, binds together by the bond
of rational sequences what the constitution
of his mind disinclined him to receive as an
arbitrary and unexplained succession. (5)
Artificial bonds of association may also sometimes be found useful, as when a schoolboy
remembers that Abydos is on the Asiatic coast
of the Hellespont, because both Asia and
Abydos commence with the letter A ; but such
tricks suit rather the necessities of an ill-trained
governess than the uses of a manly mind. I
have no faith in the systematic use of what are
called artificial mnemonic systems ; they fill the
fancy with a set of arbitrary and ridiculous

symbols which interfere with the natural play of the faculties. Dates in history, to which this sort of machinery has been generally applied, are better recollected by the causal dependence, or even the accidental contiguity of great names, as when I recollect that Plato was twenty-nine years old when Socrates drank the hemlock; and that Aristotle, the pupil of this Plato, was himself the tutor of that famous son of Philip of Macedon, who with his conquering hosts caused the language of Socrates and Plato to shake hands with the sacred dialect of the Brahmanic hymns on the banks of the Indus. (6) Lastly, whatever facilities of memory a man may possess, let him not despise the sure aids so amply supplied by written record. To speak from a paper certainly does not strengthen, but has rather a tendency to enfeeble the memory; but to retain stores of readily available matter, in the shape of written or printed record, enables a man to command a vast amount of accumulated materials, at whatever moment he may require them. In this view the young student cannot begin too early the practice of interleaving certain books, and making a good index to others, or in some such fashion tabulating his knowledge for apt and easy reference. Our preachers would certainly much increase the value of their weekly discourses if they would keep interleaved Bibles, and insert at apposite and striking texts such facts in life, or anecdotes from books, as might tend to their illustration. They might thus, even with a very weak natural memory, learn to bring forth from their treasury things new and old, with a wealth of practical application in those parts of their spiritual addresses which are at present generally the most meagre and the most vague. By political students Aristotle's *Politics* might be beneficially interleaved in the same way, and the mind thus preserved from that rigidity and one-sidedness which a familiarity with only the most modern and recent experience of public life is so apt to engender.

IX. A most important matter, not seldom neglected in the scholastic and academical training of young men, is the art of polished, pleasant, and effective expression. I shall therefore offer a few remarks here on the formation of STYLE, and on PUBLIC SPEAKING. Man is naturally a speaking animal; and a good style is merely that accomplishment in the art of verbal expression which arises from the improvement of the natural faculty by good training. The best training for the formation of style is of course familiar intercourse with good speakers and writers. A man's vocabulary depends very much always, and in the first stages perhaps altogether, on the company he keeps. Read, therefore, the best compositions of the most lofty-minded and eloquent men, and you will not fail to catch something of their nobility, only let there be no slavish imitation of any man's manner of expression. There is a certain individuality about every man's style, as about his features, which must be preserved. Also, be not over anxious about mere style, as if it were a thing that could be cultivated independently of ideas. Be more careful that you should have something weighty and pertinent to say, than that you should say things in the most polished and skilful way. There is good sense in what Socrates said to the clever young Greeks in this regard, that if they had something to say they would know how to say it; and to the same effect spoke St. Paul to the early Corinthian Christians, and in these last times the wise Goethe to the German students—

> "Be thine to seek the honest gain,
> No shallow-sounding fool;
> Sound sense finds utterance for itself,
> Without the critic's rule;
> If to your heart your tongue be true,
> Why hunt for words with much ado?"

But with this reservation you cannot be too diligent in acquiring the habit of expressing your thoughts on paper with that combination of lucid order, graceful ease, pregnant significance, and rich variety, which marks a good style. But for well-educated men, in this country at least, and for normally-constituted men in all countries I should say, writing is only a step to speaking. Not only professional men, such as preachers, advocates, and politicians, but almost every man in a free country, may be called upon occasionally to express his sentiments in public; and unless the habit be acquired early, in later years there is apt to be felt a certain awkwardness and difficulty in the public utterance of thought, which is not the less real because it is

in most cases artificial. The great thing here
is to begin early, and to avoid that slavery of
the paper, which, as Plato foresaw,* makes so
many cultivated men in these days less natural
in their speech, and less eloquent, than the most
untutored savages. Young men should train
themselves to marshal their ideas in good order,
and keep a firm grip of them without the help
of paper. A card, with a few leading words to
catch the eye, may help the memory in the first
place; but it is better, as often as possible, to
dispense with even this assistance. A speaker
should always look his audience directly in the
face, which he cannot do when he is obliged to
cast a side glance into a paper. In order to
acquire early this useful habit, I need scarcely
say that there is no better training school than
the debating societies which have long been a
strong point of the Scottish universities. Practice will produce dexterity; dexterity will work
confidence; and the bashfulness and timidity
so natural to a young man when first called
upon to address a public meeting, so far as it
lames and palsies his utterance, will disappear;
that it should disappear altogether is far from
necessary. Forwardness and pertness are a much
more serious fault in a young speaker than a
little nervous bashfulness. A public speaker
should never wish to shake himself free from
that feeling of responsibility which belongs to
his position as one whose words are meant to
influence, and ought to influence, the sentiments
of all ranks of his fellow beings; but that this

* See the Phædrus.

feeling of reverential respect for the virtue of the spoken word may not degenerate into a morbid anxiety, and a pale concern for tame propriety, I would advise him not to think of himself at all, but to go to the pulpit or platform with a thorough command of his subject, with an earnest desire to do some good by his talk, and to trust to God for the utterance. Of course this does not imply that in respect of distinct and effective utterance a man has nothing to learn from a professed master of elocution ; it is only meant that mere intelligible speaking is a natural thing, about which no special anxiety is to be felt. Accomplished speaking, like marching or dancing, is an art, for the exercise of which, in many cases, a special training is necessary.

X. I said under the first head that the fountains of true wisdom are not books ; nevertheless, in the present stage of society, books play, and must continue to play, a great part in the training of young minds ; and therefore I shall here set down some points in detail with regard to the choice and the use of BOOKS. Keep in mind, in the first place, that though the library-shelves groan with books, whose name is legion, there are in each department only a few great books, in relation to which others are but auxiliary, or it may be sometimes parasitical, and, like the ivy, doing harm rather than good to the bole round which they cling. How many thousands, for instance, and tens of thousands, of books on Christian theology have

been written and published in the world since
the first preaching of the Gospel, which, of
course contain nothing more and nothing better
than the Gospel itself, and which, if they were
all burnt to-morrow, would leave Christianity
in the main, nothing the worse, and in some
points essentially the better. There is fully as
much nonsense as sense in many learned books
that have made a noise in their day; and in
most books there is a great deal of superfluous
and useless talk. Stick therefore to the great
books, the original books, the fountain-heads of
great ideas and noble passions, and you will
learn joyfully to dispense with the volumes of
accessory talk by which their virtue has been
as frequently obscured as illuminated. For a
young theologian it is of far greater importance
that he should have the Greek New Testament
by heart than that he should be able to talk
glibly about the last volume of sermons by Dr.
Kerr or Stopford Brooke. All these are very
well, but they are not the one thing needful;
for the highest Christian culture they may
lightly be dispensed with. Not so the Bible.
Fix therefore in your eye the great books on
which the history of human thought and the
changes of human fortunes have turned. In
politics look to Aristotle; in mathematics to
Newton; in philosophy to Leibnitz; in theology
to Cudworth; in poetry to Shakspeare; in
science to Faraday. Cast a firm glance also on
those notable men, who, though not achieving
any valuable positive results of speculation, were
useful in their day, as protesting against wide-

spread popular error, and rousing people into trains of more consistent thinking and acting. To this class of men belonged Voltaire amongst the French, and David Hume in our country. But, of course, while you covet earnestly a familiar acquaintance with all such original thinkers and discoverers in the world of thought and action, you will feel only too painfully that you cannot always lay hold of them in the first stage of your studies; you will require steps to mount up to shake hands with these Celestials; and these steps are little books. Do not therefore despise little books; they are for you the necessary lines of approach to the great fortress of knowledge, and cannot safely be overleapt. On the contrary, take a little grammar, for instance, when learning a language, rather than a big one; and learn the fundamental things, the anatomy, the bones and solid framework, with strict accuracy, before plunging into the complex tissue of the living physiology. This may appear harsh at first, but will save you trouble afterwards. But, while you learn your little book thoroughly, you must beware of reading it by the method of mere CRAM. Some things, no doubt, there are that must be appropriated by the process of cram; but these are not the best things, and they contain no culture. Cram is a mere mechanical operation, of which a reasoning animal should be ashamed. But cramming, however often practised, is seldom necessary; it is resorted to by those specially who cannot, or who will not, learn to think. I advise you, on the contrary, whenever possible, to think before you read, or at least while you are reading. If you can find out for yourself by a little puzzling why the three angles of a triangle not only are, but, in the very nature of the thing must be, equal to two right angles, you will have done more good to your reasoning powers than if you had got the demonstrations of the whole twelve books of Euclid by heart according to the method of cram. The next advice I give you with regard to books is that you should read as much as possible systematically and chronologically. Without order things will not hang together in the mind, and the most natural and instructive order is the order of genesis and growth. Read Plutarch's great Lives, for instance, from Theseus down to Cleomenes and Aratus, in chronological sequence, and you will have a much more vital sort of Greek history in your memory than either Thirlwall or Grote can supply. But of course neither this nor any other rule can be applied in all cases without exception. The exception to systematic reading is made by predilection. If you feel a strong natural tendency towards acquainting yourself with any particular period of history, by all means make that acquaintance; only do it accurately and thoroughly. One link in the chain firmly laid hold of, will by and by through natural connection lead to others. As you advance from favourite point to point, you will find the necessity of binding them together by some strict chronological sequence. For general information a sort of random reading may be allowed occasionally; but this sort of thing has to do only with the necessary recreation or the useful furnishing of the mind, and is utterly destitute of training virtue; and such reading, to which there is great temptation in these times, is rather prejudicial than advantageous to the mind. The great scholars of the sixteenth and seventeenth centuries had not so many books as we have, but what they had they made a grand use of. Reading, in the case of mere miscellaneous readers, is like the racing of some little dog about the moor, snuffing everything and catching nothing; but a reader of the right sort finds his prototype in Jacob, who wrestled with an angel all night, and counted himself the better for the bout, though the sinew of his thigh shrank in consequence.

XI. A few remarks may be useful on strictly PROFESSIONAL READING, as opposed to reading with the view of general culture. There is a natural eagerness among young men to commence without delay their special professional work—what the Germans very significantly call *Brodstudien;* but there cannot be a doubt that in the unqualified way that young men take up this notion, it is a great mistake, as the experience of professional men and the history of professional eminence has largely proved. For, in the first place, a little reflection will teach a thoughtful youth, that what in his present stage he may be disposed to regard as useless ornaments, or even incumbrances, are often the most valuable aids and the most serviceable tools to his future professional activity. This is peculiarly the case with languages, which seem in the first place to stand in the way of a firm grasp of things, but which become more necessary to a man the more he extends the range and fastens the roots of his professional knowledge. If languages have been often overvalued, it is only when they have been looked on as an end in themselves. Their value as tools, in the hands of an intelligent thinker, can scarcely be overrated. Again, the merely professional man is always a narrow man; worse than that, he is in a sense an artificial man, a creature of technicalities and specialties, removed equally from the broad truth of nature and from the healthy influence of human converse. In society the most accomplished man of mere professional skill is often a nullity; he has sunk his humanity in his dexterity; he is a leather-dealer, and can talk only about leather; a student, and smells fustily of books, as an inveterate smoker does of tobacco. So far from rushing hastily into merely professional studies, a young man should rather be anxious to avoid the engrossing influence of what is popularly called SHOP. He will soon enough learn to know the cramping influence of purely professional occupation. Let him flap his wings lustily in an ampler region while he may;

> " Der Jüngling soll die Flügel regen
> In Lieb und Hass gewaltig sich bewegen."

But if a man will fix his mind on merely professional study, and can find no room for general culture in his soul, let him be told, that no pro fessional studies, however complete, can teach a man the whole of his profession, that the most exact professional drill will omit to teach him the most interesting and the most important part of his own business—that part, namely, where the specialty of the profession comes directly into contact with the generality of human notions and human sympathies. Of this the profession of the law furnishes an excellent example; for, while there is no art more technical, more artificial, and more removed from a fellow-feeling of humanity, than law in many of its branches, in others it marches out into the grand arena of human rights and liberties, and deals with large questions, in the handling of which it is often of more consequence that a pleader should be a complete man than that he should be an expert lawyer. In the same way, medicine has as much to do with a knowledge of human nature and of the human soul as with the virtues of cunningly mingled drugs, and the revelations of a technical diagnosis; and theology is generally then least human and least evangelical when it is most stiffly orthodox and most nicely professional. Universal experience, accordingly, has proved that the general scholar, however apparently inferior at the first start, will, in the long run, beat the special man on his own favourite ground; for the special man, from the small field of his habitual survey, can neither know the principles on which his practice rests, nor the relation of his own particular art to general human interests and general human intelligence. The best preservatives against the cramping force of merely professional study are to be found in the healthy influences of society, in travel, and in cultivating a familiarity with the great writers—specially poets and historians—whose purely human thoughts " make rich the blood of the world," and enlarge the platform of sympathetic intelligence.

XII. I will conclude this chapter of intellectual culture with some remarks on a subject with regard to which, considering my professional position, people will naturally be inclined to expect, and willing to receive advice from me —I mean the study of LANGUAGES. The short rules which I will set down in what appears to me their order of natural succession, are the result of many years' experience, and may be relied on as being of a strictly practical character.

(1.) If possible always start with a good teacher. He will save you much time by clearing away difficulties that might otherwise discourage you, and preventing the formation of bad habits of enunciation, which must afterwards be unlearned.

(2.) The next step is to name aloud, in the language to be learned, every object which meets your eye, carefully excluding the intervention of the English: in other words, think and speak of the objects about you in the language you are learning from the very first hour of your teaching; and remember that the language belongs in the first place to your ear and to your tongue, not in your book merely and to your brain.

(3.) Commit to memory the simplest and most normal forms of the declension of nouns, such as the *us* and *a* declension in Latin, and the A declension in Sanscrit.

(4.) The moment you have learned the nominative and accusative cases of these nouns take the first person of the present indicative of any common verb, and pronounce aloud some short sentence according to the rules of syntax belonging to active verbs, as—ὁρῶ τὸν "Ηλιον, *I see the sun.*

(5.) Enlarge this practice by adding some epithet to the substantive, declined according to the same noun, as—ὁρῶ τὸν λαμπρὸν "Ηλιον, *I see the bright sun.*

(6.) Go on in this manner progressively, committing to memory the whole present indicative, past and future indicative, of simple verbs, always making short sentences with them, and some appropriate nouns, and always thinking directly in the foreign language, excluding the intrusion of the English. In this essential element of every rational system of linguistic training there is no real, but only an imaginary difficulty to contend with, and, in too many cases, the pertinacity of a perverse practice.

(7.) When the ear and tongue have acquired a fluent mastery of the simpler forms of nouns, verbs, and sentences, then, but not till then, should the scholar be led, by a graduated process, to the more difficult and complex forms.

(8.) Let nothing be learned from rules that is not immediately illustrated by practice; or rather, let the rules be educed from the practice of ear and tongue, and let them be as few and as comprehensive as possible.

(9.) Irregularities of various kinds are best learned by practice as they occur; but some anomalies, as in the conjugation of a few irregular verbs, are of such frequent occurrence, and are so necessary for progress, that they had better be learned specially by heart as soon as possible. Of this the verb to *be*, in almost all languages, is a familiar example.

(10.) Let some easy narrative be read, in the first place, or better, some familiar dialogue, as, in Greek, Xenophon's Anabasis and Memorabilia, Cebetis Tabula, and Lucian's Dialogues; but reading must never be allowed, as is so generally the case, to be practised as a substitute for thinking and speaking. To counteract this tendency, the best way is to take objects of natural history, or representations of interesting objects, and describe their parts aloud in simple sentences, without the intervention of the mother tongue.

(11.) Let all exercises of reading and describing be repeated again, and again, and again. No book fit to be read in the early stages of language-learning should be read only once.

(12.) Let your reading, if possible, be always in sympathy with your intellectual appetite. Let the matter of the work be interesting, and you will make double progress. To know something of the subject beforehand will be an immense help. For this reason, with Christians who know the Scriptures, as we do in Scotland, a translation of the Bible is always one of the best books to use in the acquisition of a foreign tongue.

(13.) As you read, note carefully the difference between the idioms of the strange language and those of the mother tongue; underscore these distinctly with pen or pencil, in some thoroughly idiomatic translation, and after a few days translate back into the original tongue what you have before you in the English form.

(14.) To methodise, and, if necessary, correct your observations, consult some systematic grammar so long as you may find it profitable. But the grammar should, as much as possible, follow the practice, not precede it.

(15.) Be not content with that mere methodical generalisation of the practice which you find in many grammars, but endeavour always to find the principle of the rule, whether belonging to universal or special grammar.

(16.) Study the theory of language, the organism of speech, and what is called comparative philology or Glossology. The principles there revealed will enable you to prosecute with a reasoning intelligence a study which would otherwise be in a great measure a laborious exercise of arbitrary memory.

(17.) Still, practice is the main thing; language must, in the first place, be familiar; and this familiarity can be attained only by constant reading and constant conversation. Where a man has no person to speak to he may declaim to himself; but the ear and the tongue must be trained, not the eye merely and the understanding. In reading, a man must not confine himself to standard works. He must devour everything greedily that he can lay his hands on. He must not merely get up a book with accurate precision; that is all very well as a special task; but he must learn to live largely in the general element of the language; and minute accuracy in details is not to be sought before a fluent practical command of the general currency of the language has been attained. Shakspeare, for instance, ought to be read twenty times before a man begins to occupy himself with the various readings of the Shaksperian text, or the ingenious conjectures of his critics.

(18.) Composition, properly so called, is the culmination of the exercises of speaking and reading, translation and re-translation, which we have sketched. In this exercise the essential thing is to write from a model, not from dictionaries or phrase-books. Choose an author who is a pattern of a particular style—say Plato in philosophical dialogue, or Lucian in playful colloquy—steal his phrases, and do something of the same kind yourself, directly, without the intervention of the English. After you have acquired fluency in this way you may venture to put more of yourself into the style, and learn to write the foreign tongue as gracefully as Latin was written by Erasmus, Wyttenbach, or Ruhnken. Translation from English classics may also be practised, but not in the first place; the ear must be tuned by direct imitation of the foreign tongue, before the more difficult art of transference from the mother tongue can be attempted with success.

ON PHYSICAL CULTURE

"The glory of a young man is his strength."
SOLOMON

ON PHYSICAL CULTURE.

I. It is a patent fact, as certain as anything in mathematics, that whatever exists must have a basis on which to stand, a root from which to grow, a hinge on which to turn, a something which, however subordinate in itself with reference to the complete whole, is the indispensable point of attachment from which the existence of the whole depends. No house can be raised except on a foundation, a substructure which has no independent virtue, and which, when it exists in the greatest perfection, is generally not visible, but rather loves to hide itself in darkness. Now this is exactly the sort of relation which subsists between a man's thinking faculty and his body, between his mental activity and his bodily health; and it is obvious that, if this analogy be true, there is nothing that a student ought to be more careful about than the sound condition of his flesh and blood. It is, however, a well-known fact that the care of their health, or, what is the same thing, the rational treatment of their own flesh and blood, is the very last thing that students seriously think of; and the more eager the student, the more apt is he to sin in this respect, and to drive himself, like an unsignalled railway train, to the very brink of a fatal precipice, before he knows where he stands. It is wise, therefore, to start in a studious life with the assured conviction which all experience warrants, that sedentary occupations generally, and specially sedentary habits combined with severe and persistent brain exercise, are more or less unhealthy, and, in the case of naturally frail constitutions, such as have frequently a tendency to fling themselves into books, tend directly to the enfeebling of the faculties and the undermining of the frame. After this warning from an old student, let every man consider that his blood shall be on his own head if he neglect to use, with a firm purpose, as much care in the preservation of his health as any good workman would do in keeping his tools sharp, or any good soldier in having his powder dry. Meanwhile I will jot down, under a few heads, some of the most important practical suggestions with which experience has furnished me in this matter.

II. The growth and vigorous condition of every member of the body, as, in fact, of every function of existence in the universe, depends on EXERCISE. All life is an energising or a working; absolute rest is found only in the grave; and the measure of a man's vitality is the measure of his working power. To possess every faculty and function of the body in harmonious working order is to be healthy; to be healthy, with a high degree of vital force, is to be strong. A man may be healthy without being strong; but all health tends, more or less, towards strength, and all disease is weakness. Now, any one may see in nature, that things grow big simply by growing; this growth is a constant and habitual exercise of vital or vegetative force, and whatever checks or diminishes the action of this force—say, harsh winds or frost—will stop the growth and stunt the production. Let the student therefore bear in mind, that sitting on a chair, leaning over a desk, poring over a book, cannot possibly be the way to make his body grow. The blood can be made to flow, and the muscles to play freely, only by exercise; and, if that exercise is not taken, Nature will not be mocked. Every young student ought to make a sacred resolution to move about in the open air at least two hours every day. If he does not do this, cold feet, the clogging of the wheels of the internal parts of the fleshly frame, and various shades of stomachic and cerebral discomfort, will not fail in due season to inform him that he has been sinning against Nature, and, if he does not amend his courses, as a bad boy he will certainly be flogged; for Nature is never, like some soft-hearted human masters, over-merciful in her treatment. But why should a student indulge so much in the lazy and unhealthy habit of sitting? A man may think as well standing as sitting, often not a little better; and as for reading in these days, when the most weighty books may be had cheaply, in the lightest form, there is no necessity why a person should be bending his back, and doubling his chest, merely because he happens to have a book in his hand. A man will read a play or a poem far more naturally and effectively while walking up and down the room, than when sitting sleepily in a chair. Sitting, in fact, is a slovenly habit, and ought not to be indulged. But when a man does sit, or must sit, let him at all events sit erect, with his back to the light, and a full free projection of the breast. Also, when studying languages, or reading fine passages of poetry, let him read as much as possible aloud; a practice recommended by Clemens of Alexandria,* and which will have the double good effect of strengthening that most important vital element the lungs, and training the ear to the perception of vocal distinctions, so stupidly neglected in many of our public schools. There is, in fact, no necessary connection, in most cases, between the knowledge which a student is anxious to acquire, and the sedentary habits which students are so apt to cultivate. A certain part of his work, no doubt, must be done amid books; but if I wish to know Homer, for instance, thoroughly, after the first grammatical and lexicographical drudgery is over, I can read him as well on the top of Ben Cruachan, or, if the day be blasty, amid the grand silver pines at Inverawe, as in a fusty study. A man's enjoyment of an Æschylean drama or a Platonic dialogue will not be diminished, but sensibly increased, by the fragrant breath of birches blow-

* πολλοῖς δὲ ἐσθ' ὅτε καὶ τὸ γεγωνὸν
τῆς ἀναγνώσεως γυμνάσιόν ἐστιν. — Pædagog. iii. 10.

ing around him, or the sound of mighty waters rushing near. As for a lexicon, if you make yourself at the first reading a short index of the more difficult words, you can manage the second reading more comfortably without it What a student should specially see to, both in respect of health and of good taste, is not to carry the breath of books with him wherever he goes, as some people carry the odour of tobacco. To prevent this contagion of bookishness, the best thing a young man can do is to join a volunteer corps, the drill connected with which will serve the double purpose of brushing off all taint of pedantry, and girding the loins stoutly for all the duties that belong to citizenship and active manhood. The modern Prussians, like the ancient Greeks, understand the value of military drill, and make every man serve his time in the army; but we rush prematurely into the shop, and our citizenship and our manhood suffer accordingly. The cheapness of railway and steamboat travelling, also, in the present day, renders inexcusable the conduct of the studious youth who will sit, week after week, and month after month, chained to a dull gray book, when he might inhale much more healthy imaginings from the vivid face of nature in some green glen or remote wave-plashed isle. A book, of course, may always be in his pocket, if a book be necessary; but it is better to cultivate independence of these paper helps, as often as may be, to learn directly from observation of nature, and to sit in a frame of "wise passiveness," growing insensibly in strong thought and feeling, by the breezy influences of Nature playing about us. But it is not necessary that a man should be given to indulge in Wordsworthian musings, before the modern habits of travelling and touring can be made to subserve the double end of health and culture. Geology, Botany, Zoology, and all branches of Natural History, are best studied in the open air; and their successful cultivation necessarily implies the practice of those habits of active and enterprising pedestrianism, which are such a fine school of independent manhood. History also and archæology are most aptly studied in the storied glen, the ruined abbey, or the stout old border tower; and in fact, in an age when the whole world is more or less locomotive, the student who stays at home, and learns in a gray way only from books, in addition to the prospect of dragging through life with enfeebled health, and dropping into a premature grave, must make up his mind to be looked on by all well-conditioned persons as a weakling and an oddity.

For keeping the machine of the body in a fine poise of flexibility and firmness, nothing deserves a higher place than GAMES and GYMNASTICS. A regular constitutional walk, as it is called, before dinner, as practised by many persons, has no doubt something formal about it, which not everybody knows to season with pleasantness: to those who feel the pressure of such formality, athletic games supply the necessary exercise along with a healthy social stimulus. For boys and young men, cricket; for persons of a quiet temperament, and staid

ON PHYSICAL CULTURE.   15

old bachelors, bowls; for all persons and all ages, the breezy Scottish game of golf is to be commended. Boating of course, when not overdone, as it sometimes is in Oxford and Cambridge, is a manly and characteristically British exercise; and the delicate management of sail and rudder as practised in the Shetland and Hebridean seas, is an art which calls into play all the powers that belong to a prompt and vigorous manhood. Angling, again, is favourable to musing and poetic imaginings, as the examples of Walton and Stoddart, and glorious John Wilson, largely show; in rainy weather billiards is out of sight the best game; in it there is developed a quickness of eye, an expertness of touch, and a subtlety of calculation, truly admirable. In comparison with this cards are stupid, which, at best, in whist, only exercise the memory, while chess can scarcely be called an amusement; it is a study, and a severe brain exercise, which for a man of desultory mental activity may have a bracing virtue, but to a systematic thinker can scarcely act as a relief.

III. Let me now make a few remarks on the very vulgar, but by no means always wisely managed process of EATING and DRINKING. Abernethy was wont to say that the two great killing powers in the world are STUFF and FRET. Of these the former certainly has nothing to do with the premature decay of Scottish students; they die rather of eating too little than of eating too much. Of course it is necessary, in the first place, that you should have something to eat, and, in the second place, that what you eat should be substantial and nourishing. With regard to the details of this matter you must consult the doctor; but I believe it is universally agreed that the plainest food is often the best; and for the highest cerebral and sanguineous purposes, long experience has proved that there is nothing better than oatmeal and good pottage. For as the poet says—

> " Buirdly chiels and clever hizzies
> Are bred in sic a way as this is."

Supposing, however, that the supply of good nourishment is adequate, people are apt to err in various ways when they come to use it. There is a class of people who do not walk through life, but race; they do not know what it is to sit down to anything with a quiet purpose, and so they bolt their dinner with a galloping purpose to be done with it as soon as possible. This is bad policy and bad philosophy. The man who eats in a hurry loses both the pleasure of eating and the profit of digestion. If men of business in bustling cities, and Americans who live in a constant fever of democratic excitement, are apt to indulge in this unhealthy habit, students and bookish men are not free from the same temptation. Eager readers will not only bolt their dinner that they may get to their books, but they will read sometimes even while they are eating; thus forcing nature to act from two distinct vital centres at the same time—the brain and the stomach—of which the necessary result is to enfeeble both. To sip a cup of tea with Lucian or Aristophanes in one hand may be both pleasant and profitable; but dinner is a more serious affair, and must be gone about with a devotion of the whole man—*totus in illis*, " a whole man to one thing at one time," as Chancellor Thurlow said, —seasoned very properly, with agreeable conversation or a little cheerful music, where you can have it, but never mingled with severe cogitations or perplexing problems. In this view the custom of the English and German students of dining with one another, is much to be commended before the solitary feeding too often practised by poor Scottish students in lonely lodging houses. In this matter the Free Church of Scotland, among its other notable achievements, has recently shown us an example well worthy of imitation. They have instituted a dining hall for their theological students, distinguished by salubrity, cheapness, and sociality. Next to quality, a certain variety of food is by all means to be sought after. The stimulus of novelty that goes along with variety, sharpens appetite; besides that Nature, in all her rich and beautiful ways, emphatically protests against monotony. It is, moreover, a point of practical wisdom to prevent the stomach from becoming the habituated slave of any kind of food. In change of circumstances the favourite diet cannot always be had : and so, to keep himself in a state of alimentary comfort, your methodical eater must restrict his habits of locomotion, and narrow the range of his existence to a fixed sphere where he can be fed regularly with his meted portion. As for drink, I need not say that a glass of good beer or wine is always pleasant, and in certain cases may even be necessary to stimulate digestion; but healthy young men can never require such stimulus; and the more money that a poor Scotch student can spare from unnecessary and slippery luxuries, such as drink and tobacco, so much the better. "Honest water" certainly has this merit, that it "never made any man a sinner;" and of whisky it may be said that, however beneficial it may be on a wet moor or on the top of a frosty Ben in the Highlands, when indulged in habitually it never made any man either fair or fat. He who abstains from it altogether will never die in a ditch, and will always find a penny in his pocket to help himself and his friend in an emergency.

IV. I believe there are few things more necessary than to warn students against the evil effects of close rooms and bad ventilation. Impure air can never make pure blood; and impure blood corrupts the whole system. But the evil is, that, no immediate sensible effects being produced from a considerable amount of impurity in the air, thoughtless and careless persons—that is, I am afraid, the great majority of persons—go on inhaling it without receiving any hint that they are imbibing poison. But those evils are always the most dangerous of which the approaches are the most insidious.

Let students, therefore, who are often confined in small rooms, be careful to throw open their windows whenever they go out; and, if the windows of their sleeping-room are so situated that they can be kept open without sending a draught of air directly across the sleeper, let them by all means be left open night and day, both summer and winter. In breezy Scotland, at least, this practice, except in the case of very sensitive subjects, can only be beneficial. In hot countries, where insalubrious vapours in some places infest the night, it may be otherwise.

V. Should it be necessary to say a word about SLEEP? One would think not. Nature, we may imagine, is sufficient for herself in this matter. Let a man sleep when he is sleepy, and rise when the crow of the cock, or the glare of the sun, rouses him from his torpor. Exactly so, if Nature always got fair play; but she is swindled and flouted in so many ways by human beings, that a general reference to her often becomes a useless generality. In the matter of sleep specially students are great sinners; nay, their very profession is a sin against repose; and the strictest prophylactic measures are necessary to prevent certain poaching practices of thinking men into the sacred domain of sleep. Cerebral excitement, like strong coffee, is the direct antagonist of sleep; therefore the student should so apportion his hours of intellectual task-work, that the more exciting and stimulating brain exercise should never be continued direct into the hour for repose; but let the last work of the day be always something comparatively light and easy, or dull and soporific; or better still, let a man walk for an hour before bed, or have a pleasant chat with a chum, and then there can be no fear but that nature, left to herself, will find, without artifice, the measure of rest which she requires. As to the exact amount of that measure, no rule can be laid down; less than six, or more than eight hours' sleep, according to general experience, must always be exceptional. The student who walks at least two hours every day, and works hard with his brain eight or nine hours besides, will soon find out what is the natural measure of sleep that he requires, to keep free from the feverishness and the languor that are the necessary consequences of prolonged artificial wakefulness. As to early rising, which makes such a famous figure in some notable biographies, I can say little about it, as it is a virtue which I was never able to practise. There can be no doubt, however, that, wherever it can be practised in a natural and easy way, it is a very healthful practice; and in certain circumstances, such as those in which the late distinguished Baron Bunsen was placed, full of various business and distraction, the morning hours seem clearly to be pointed out as the only ones available for the purposes of learned research and devout meditation.

VI. On the use of BATHS and WATER as a hygienic instrument I can speak with confidence, as I have frequented various celebrated hydropathic institutions, and have carefully pondered both the principles and the practice of that therapeutic discipline. Hydropathy is a name that very inadequately expresses the virtue of the treatment to which it subjects the patient. It is a well-calculated combination of exercise, leisure, diet, amusement, society, and water, applied in various ways to stimulate the natural perspiratory action of the skin. Any one may see that the influences brought to bear on the bodily system by such a combination are in the highest degree sanitary. The important point for students is to be informed that parts of this discipline somewhat expensively pursued in hydropathic institutions under the superintendence of experienced physicians, can be transferred safely, and at no expense, to the routine of their daily life. A regular bath in the morning, where water can be had, unless with very feeble and delicate subjects, has always an invigorating effect ; but, where water is scarce, a wet sheet, dipped in water, and well wrung, will serve the purpose equally well. The body must be altogether enveloped, and well rubbed with this ; and then a dry sheet used in the same way will cause a glow to come out in the skin, which is the best preventive against those disturbances of cuticular action which the instability of our northern climate renders so common and so annoying. The wet sheet packing, one of the most bruited of the hydropathic appliances, and which in fact acts as a mild tepid blister swathing the whole body, may be practised for special purposes, under the direction of a person expert in those matters; but the virtue of this, as of all water applications, depends on the power of reaction which the physical system possesses. This reaction young men of good constitutions, trained by healthy exercise and exposure, will always possess; but persons of a dull and slow temperament should beware of making sudden experiments with cold water without certain precautions and directions from those who are more experienced than themselves.

VII. What I have further to say about health belongs to an altogether different chapter. A man cannot be kept healthy merely by attending to his stomach. If the body, which is the support of the curiously complex fabric, acts with a sustaining influence on the mind, the mind, which is the impelling force of the machine, may, like steam in a steam-engine, for want of a controlling and regulative force, in a single fit of untempered expansion, blow all the wheels and pegs, and close compacted plates of the machine, into chaos. No function of the body can be safely performed for a continuance without the habitual strong control of a well-disciplined will. All merely physical energies in man have a strong tendency to run riot into fever and dissolution when divorced from the superintendence of what Plato called Imperial mind (βασιλικὸς νοῦς). The music of well-regulated emotions imparts its harmony to the strings of the physical machine; and freedom from the blind plunges of wilfulness keeps the heart free from those fierce and irregular beatings which wear out its vitality prematurely. Therefore, if you would be healthy, be good; and if you would be good, be wise; and if you would be wise, be devout and reverent, for the fear of God is the beginning of wisdom. What this means it will be the business of the following chapter to set forth.

ON MORAL CULTURE.

Μέγας γὰρ ὁ ἀγών, μέγας, οὐχ ὅσος δοκεῖ, τὸ χρηστὸν ἢ κακὸν γενέσθαι.

PLATO.

ON MORAL CULTURE.

I. We are now come to the most important of the three great chapters of self-culture. The moral nature of man supplies him both with the motive and the regulative power, being in fact the governor, and lord, and legitimate master of the whole machine. Moral excellence is therefore justly felt to be an indispensable element in all forms of human greatness. A man may be as brilliant, as clever, as strong, and as broad as you please: and with all this, if he is not good, he may be a paltry fellow; and even the sublime which he seems to reach, in his most splendid achievements, is only a brilliant sort of badness. The first Napoleon, in his thunderous career over our western world, was a notable example of superhuman force in a human shape, without any real human greatness. It does not appear that he was naturally what we should call a bad man; but, devoting himself altogether to military conquest and political ascendency, he had no occasion to exercise any degree of that highest excellence which grows out of unselfishness, and so, as a moral man, he lived and died very poor and very small. But it is not only conquerors and politicians that, from a defect of the moral element, fail to achieve real greatness. "Nothing," says Hartley, "can easily exceed the vain-glory, self-conceit, arrogance, emulation, and envy, that are to be found in the eminent professors of the sciences, mathematics, natural philosophy, and even divinity itself."* Nor is there any reason to be astonished at this. The moral nature, like everything else, if it is to grow into any sort of excellence, demands a special culture; and, as our passions, by their very nature, like the winds, are not easy of control, and our actions are the outcome of our passions, it follows that moral excellence will in no case be an easy affair, and in its highest grades will be the most arduous, and, as such, the most noble achievement of a thoroughly accomplished humanity. It was an easy thing for Lord Byron to be a great poet; it was merely indulging his nature; he was an eagle, and must fly; but to have curbed his wilful humour, soothed his fretful discontent, and learned to behave like a reasonable being and a gentleman, that was a difficult matter, which he does not seem ever seriously to have attempted. His life, therefore, with all his genius, and fits of occasional sublimity, was, on the whole, a terrible failure, and a great warning to all who are willing to take a lesson. Another flaring beacon of the rock, on which great wits are often wrecked for want of a little kindly cul-

---

* "Observations on Man." London, 1749. Vol. ii. p. 225.

ture of unselfishness, is Walter Savage Landor, the most finished master of style, perhaps, that ever used the English tongue; but a person at the same time so imperiously wilful, and so majestically cross-grained, that, with all his polished style and pointed thought, he was constantly living on the verge of insanity. Let every one, therefore, who would not suffer shipwreck on the great voyage of life, stamp seriously into his soul, before all things, the great truth of the Scripture text,—" ONE THING IS NEEDFUL." Money is not needful; power is not needful; cleverness is not needful; fame is not needful; liberty is not needful; even health is not the one thing needful: but character alone — a thoroughly cultivated will — is that which can truly save us; and, if we are not saved in this sense, we must certainly be damned. There is no point of indifference in this matter, where a man can safely rest, saying to himself, If I don't get better, I shall certainly not get worse. He will unquestionably get worse. The unselfish part of his nature, if left uncultivated, will, like every other neglected function, tend to shrink into a more meagre vitality and more stunted proportions. Let us gird up our loins, therefore, and quit us like men; and, having by the golden gift of God the glorious lot of living once for all, let us endeavour to live nobly.

II. It may be well, before entering into any detail, to indicate, in a single word, the connection between morality and piety, which is not always correctly understood. A certain school of

British moralists, from Jeremy Bentham downwards, have set themselves to tabulate a scheme of morals without any reference to religion, which, to say the least of it, is a very unnatural sort of divorce, and a plain sign of a certain narrowness and incompleteness in the mental constitution of those who advocate such views. No doubt a professor of wisdom, like old Epicurus, may be a very good man, as the world goes, and lead a very clean life, believing that all the grand mathematical structure of this magnificent universe is the product of a mere fortuitous concourse of blind atoms; as, in these days, I presume, there are few more virtuous men than some who talk of laws of Nature, invariable sequence, natural selection, favourable conditions, happy combination of external circumstances, and other such reasonless phrases as may seem to explain the frame of the universe apart from mind. But to a healthy human feeling there must always be something very inadequate, say rather something abnormal and monstrous, in this phasis of morality. It is as if a good citizen in a monarchy were to pay all the taxes conscientiously, serve his time in the army, and fight the battles of his country bravely, but refuse to take off his hat to the Queen when she passed. If we did not note such a fellow altogether with a black mark, as a disloyal and disaffected subject, we should feel a good-natured contempt for him, as a crotchety person and unmannerly. So it is exactly with atheists, whether speculative or practical; they are mostly crotchet-mongers and puzzle-brains; fellows who spin silken ropes in which to strangle themselves; at most, mere reasoning machines, utterly devoid of every noble inspiration, whose leaden intellectual firmament has no heat and no colour, whose whole nature is exhausted in fostering a prim self-contained conceit about their petty knowledges, and who can, in fact, fasten their coarse feelers upon nothing but what they can finger, and classify, and tabulate, and dissect. But there is something that stands above all fingering, all microscopes, and all curious diagnosis, and that is, simply, LIFE ; and life is simply energising Reason, and energising Reason is only another name for GOD. To ignore this supreme fact is to attempt to conceive the steam-engine without the intellect of James Watt; it is to make a map of the aqueducts that supply a great city with water, without indicating the fountainhead from which they are supplied; it is to stop short of the one fact which renders all the other facts possible ; it is to leave the body without the head. By no means, therefore, let a young man satisfy himself with any of those cold moral schemes of the present age of reaction, which piece together a beggarly account of duties from external induction. The fountain of all the nobler morality is moral inspiration from within ; and the feeder of this fountain is GOD.

III. I will now specialise a few of those virtues the attainment of which should be an object of lofty ambition to young men desirous of making the most of the divine gift of life.

Every season and every occasion makes its own imperious demand, and presents its peculiar opportunity of glorious victory or ignoble defeat in the great battle of existence. Primroses grow only in the spring; and certain virtues, if they do not put forth vigorous shoots in youth, are not likely to show any luxuriant leafage in after age.

IV. First, there is OBEDIENCE. There is a great talk in these days about liberty; and no doubt liberty is a very good thing, and highly estimated by all healthy creatures; but it is necessary that we should understand exactly what this thing means. It means only that in the exercise of all natural energies, each creature shall be free from every sort of conventional, artificial, and painful restriction. Such liberty is unquestionably an unqualified good, but it does not bring a man very far. It fixes only the starting-point in the race of life. It gives a man a stage to play on, but it says nothing of the part he has to play, or of the style in which he must play it. Beyond this necessary starting-point, all further action in life, so far from being liberty, is only a series of limitations. All regulation is limitation; and regulation is only another name for reasoned existence. And, as the regulations to which men must submit are not always or generally those which they have willingly laid down for themselves, but rather for the most part those which have been laid down by others for the general good of society, it follows, that whosoever will be a good member of any social system must learn, in the first place, to OBEY. The law, the army, the church, the state service, every field of life and every sphere of action, are only the embodied illustrations of this principle. Freedom, of course, is left to the individual in his own individual sphere. To leave him no freedom were to make him a mere machine, and to annihilate his humanity; but, so far as he acts in a social capacity, he cannot be free from the limitations that bind the whole into a definite and consistent unity. He may be at the very top of the social ladder, but, like the Pope—SERVUS SERVORUM—only the more a slave for that. The brain can no more disown the general laws of the organism than the foot can. The loyal obedience of each member is at once its duty and its safety. St. Paul, with his usual force, fervour, and sagacity, has grandly illustrated this text; and if you ever feel inclined fretfully to kick against your special function in the great social organism, I advise you to make a serious reading of 1 Cor. xii. 14-31. Every random or wilful move is a chink opened in the door, which, if it be taught to gape wider, will in due season let in chaos. The Roman historian records it as a notable trait in the great Punic captain's character, that he knew equally well to obey and to command, —" *Nunquam ingenium idem ad res diversissimas, parendum atque imperandum habilius fuit.*" Opposite things, no doubt, obedience and command are; but the one, nevertheless, is the best training-school for the other; for he who has been accustomed only to command will not know the limitations by which, for its own beneficial exercise, all authority is bound. Let the old Roman submission to authority be cultivated by all young men as a virtue at once most characteristically social, and most becoming in unripe years. Let the thing commanded by a superior authority be done simply because it is commanded, and let it be done with punctuality. Nothing commends a young man so much to his employers as accuracy and punctuality in the conduct of business. And no wonder. On each man's exactitude in doing his special best depends the comfortable and easy going of the whole machine. In the complicated tasks of social life no genius and no talent can compensate for the lack of obedience. If the clock goes fitfully, nobody knows the time of day; and, if your allotted task is a necessary link in the chain of another man's work, you are his clock, and he ought to be able to rely on you. The greatest praise that can be given to the member of any association is in these terms:—*This is a man who always does what is required of him, and who always appears at the hour when he is expected to appear.*

V. The next grand virtue which a young man should specially cultivate is TRUTHFULNESS. I believe, with Plato, that a lie is a thing naturally hateful both to gods and men; and young persons specially are naturally truthful; but fear and vanity, and various influences, and interests affecting self, may check and overgrow this instinct, so as to produce a very hollow and worthless manhood. John Stuart Mill, in one of his political pamphlets, told the working classes of England that they were mostly liars; and yet he paid them the compliment of saying that they were the only working class in Europe who were inwardly ashamed of the baseness which they practised. A young man in his first start of life should impress on his mind strongly that he lives in a world of stern realities, where no mere show can permanently assert itself as substance. In his presentment as a member of society he should take a sacred care to be more than he seems, not to seem more than he is. Οὐ γὰρ δοκεῖν ἄριστος ἀλλ' εἶναι θέλει. Whoever in any special act is studious to make an outward show, to which no inward substance corresponds, is acting a lie, which may help him out of a difficulty perhaps for the occasion, but, like silvered copper, will be found out in due season. Plated work will never stand the tear and wear of life like the genuine metal; believe this. What principally induces men to act this sort of social lie is, with persons in trade, love of gain; but with young men, to whom I now speak, either laziness, vanity, or cowardice; and against these three besetting sins, therefore, a young man should set a special guard. Lazy people are never ready with the right article when it is wanted, and accordingly they present a false one, as when a schoolboy, when called upon to translate a passage from a Greek or Latin author, reads from a translation on the opposite page. What is this but a lie? The teacher wishes to know what you have in your brain, and you give him what you take from a piece of paper, not the produce of your brain at all. All flimsy, shallow, and superficial work, in fact, is a LIE, of which a man ought to be ashamed. Vanity is another provocative of lies. From a desire to appear well before others, young men, who are naturally ignorant and inexperienced, will sometimes be tempted to pretend that they know more than they actually do know, and may thus get into a habit of dressing up their little with the air and attitude of much, in such a manner as to convey a false impression of their own importance. Let a man learn as early as possible honestly to confess his ignorance, and he will be a gainer by it in the long run ; otherwise the trick by which he veils his ignorance from others may become a habit by which he conceals it from himself, and learns to spend his whole life in an element of delusive show, to which no reality corresponds. But it is from deficiency of courage rather than from the presence of vanity that a young man may expect to be most sorely tried. Conceit, which is natural to youth, is sure to be pruned down ; the whole of society is in a state of habitual conspiracy to lop the overweening self-estimate of any of its members ; but a little decent cowardice is always safe ; and those who begin life by being afraid to speak what they think, are likely to end it by being afraid to think what they wish. Moral courage is unquestionably, if the most manly, certainly the rarest of the social virtues.

The most venerated traditions and institutions of society, and even some of the kindliest and most finely-fibred affections, are in not a few cases arrayed against its exercise ; and in such cases to speak the truth boldly requires a combination of determination and of tact, of which not every man is capable. Neither, indeed, is it desirable always to speak all the truth that a man may happen to know ; there is no more offensive thing than truth, when it runs counter to certain great social interests, associations, and passions ; and offence, though it must sometimes be given, ought never to be courted. To these matters the text applies, " Be ye wise as serpents and harmless as doves." Nevertheless there are occasions when a man must speak boldly out, even at the risk of plucking the beard of fair authority somewhat rudely. If he does not do so he is a coward and a poltroon, and not the less so because he has nine hundred and ninety-nine lily-livered followers at his back.

VI. I don't know a better advice to a young man than NEVER TO BE IDLE. It is one of those negative sort of precepts that impart no motive force to the will ; but though negations seem barren to keep out the devil by a strong bolt, they may prove in the end not the worst receipt for admitting the good spirit into confidence. A man certainly should not circumscribe his activity by any inflexible fence of rigid rules ; such a formal methodism of conduct springs from narrowness, and can only end in more narrowness; but it is of the utmost importance to commence early with an œconomical use of time, and this is only possible by means of order and system. No young person can go far wrong who devotes a certain amount of time regularly to a definite course of work: how much that portion of time should be, of course depends on circumstances; but let it, at all events, be filled up with a prescribed continuity of something; one hour a day persistently devoted to one thing, like a small seed, will yield a large increase at the year's end. Random activity, jumping from one thing to another without a plan, is little better, in respect of any valuable intellectual result, than absolute idleness. An idle man is like a housekeeper who keeps the doors open for any burglar. It is a grand safeguard when a man can say, I have no time for nonsense; no call for unreasonable dissipation; no need for that sort of stimulus which wastes itself in mere titillation; variety of occupation is my greatest pleasure, and when my task is finished I know how to lie fallow, and with soothing rest prepare myself for another bout of action. The best preventive against idleness is to start with the deep-seated conviction of the earnestness of life. Whatever men say of the world, it is certainly no stage for trifling; in a scene where all are at work idleness can lead only to wreck and ruin. " LIFE IS SHORT, ART LONG, OPPORTUNITY FLEETING, EXPERIMENT SLIPPERY, JUDGMENT DIFFICULT." These are the first words of the medical aphorisms of the wise Hippocrates; they were set down as a significant sign at the porch of the benevolent science of healing more than 500 years before the Christian era; and they remain still, the wisest text which a man can take with him as a directory into any sphere of effective social activity.

VII. If we look around us in the world with a view to discover what is the cause of the sad deficiency of energy often put forth in the best of causes, we shall find that it arises generally from some sort of NARROWNESS. A man will not help you in this or that noble undertaking simply because he has no sympathy with it. Not a few persons are a sort of human lobsters; they live in a hard shell formed out of some professional, ecclesiastical, political, or classical crust, and cautiously creep their way within certain beaten bounds, beyond which they have no desires. The meagre and unexpansive life of such persons teaches us what we want in order to attain to a wider and a richer range of social vitality. The octogenarian poet-philosopher Goethe, when sinking into the darkness of death, called out with his last breath, MORE LIGHT! What every young man should call out daily, if he wishes to save himself from the narrowing crust of professional and other limitations, is, MORE LOVE! Men are often clever enough, but they don't know what to do with their cleverness; they are good swordsmen, but they have no cause to fight for, or prefer fighting in a bad cause. What these men want is Love. The precept of the great apostle, "*Weep with those who weep, and rejoice with those who rejoice,*" if it were grandly carried out would make every man's life as rich in universal sympathy as Shakspeare's imagination was in universal imagery. Every man cannot be a poet; but every man may give himself some trouble to cultivate that kindly and genial sensibility on which the writing and the appreciation of poetry depends. To live poetry, indeed, is always better than to write it; better for the individual, and better for society. Now a poetical life is just a life opposed to all sameness and all selfishness; eagerly seizing upon the good and beautiful from all quarters, as on its proper aliment. Let a young man, therefore, above all things, beware of shutting himself up within a certain narrow pale of sympathy, and fostering unreasonable hatreds and prejudices against others. An honest hater is often a better fellow than a cool friend; but it is better not to hate at all. A good man will as much as possible strive to be shaken out of himself, and learn to study the excellences of persons and parties to whom he is naturally opposed. It was an admirable trait in the character of the late distinguished head of the utilitarian school of ethics, who was brought up according to the strictest sect of a narrow and unsympathetic school, that he could apply himself in the spirit of kindly recognition to comprehend two such antipodal characters as Coleridge and Thomas Carlyle. Never allow yourself to indulge in sneering condemnations of large classes and sections of your fellow beings; that sort of talk sounds big, but is in fact puerile. Never refuse to entertain a man in your heart because all the world is talking against him, or because he belongs to some sect or party that everybody despises; if he is universally talked against, as has happened to many of the best men in certain circumstances, there is only so much the more need that he should receive a friendly judgment from you. "Honour all men" is one of the many texts of combined sanctity and sapience with which the New Testament abounds; but this you cannot do unless you try to know all men; and you know no man till you have looked with the eye of a brother into the best that is in him. To do this is the true moral philosophy, the best human riches; a wealth which, when you have quarried, you can proceed, as a good social architect, to build up the truth in love, with regard to all men, and make your deeds in every point as genuine as your words.

VIII. There is a class of young men in the present age on whose face one imagines that he sees written NIL ADMIRARI. This is not at all a loveable class of "the youth-head" of our land; and, unless the tone of not wondering which characterises their manner be a sort of juvenile affectation destined soon to pass away, rather a hopeless class. Wonder, as Plato has it, is a truly philosophic passion; the more we have of it, accompanying the reverent heart, of course with a clear open eye, so much the better. That it should be specially abundant in the opening scenes of life is in the healthy course of nature; and to be deficient in it argues either insensibility, or that indifference, selfishness, and conceit, which are sometimes found combined with a shallow sort of cleverness that, with superficial observers readily passes for true talent. In opposition to this most unnatural, ungenial habitude of mind, we say to every young man, cultivate REVERENCE. You will not see much of this virtue, perhaps, in the democratic exhibitions in which the present age delights; but it is the true salt of the soul for all that.

"We live by admiration, hope, and love."

We are small creatures, the biggest of us, and our only chance of becoming great in a sort is by participation in the greatness of the universe. St. John, in a beautiful passage of his First Epistle, has finely indicated the philosophy of this matter. " Beloved, now are we the sons of God ; and it doth not yet appear what we shall be; but we know that when he shall appear, we shall be like him; for we shall see him as he is ;"—that is to say, to look with admiring rapture on a type of perfect excellence is the way to become assimilated to that excellence ; what the uncorrupted man sees in such cases he admires ; and what he admires he imitates. The chief end of man, according to the Stoics, was,—" SPECTARE ET IMITARI MUNDUM!"—a fine thought, and finely expressed. But how shall a man see when he has no admiring faculty which shall lead him to see, and how shall he imitate what he does not know? All true appreciation is the result of keen insight and noble passion; but the habit of despising things and persons, and holding them cheap, blinds the one factor which belongs to the complete result, and strangles the other.

IX. In morals there are principles of inspiration and principles of regulation: love and reverence, of which we have been speaking, belong to the former; MODERATION, of which we are now to speak, belongs to the latter. It is a virtue of which young men generally have no conception, and for deficiency in which they are lightly pardoned; but it is a virtue not the less necessary for that, and if they will not learn it in what medical men call the prophylactic way, —that is, timeously, before the touch of danger, —they will have to learn it at no very long date from perilous experience. To hot young blood it is an admonition which sounds as cheap as it is distasteful, to beware of excess; but hot young blood, which knows well enough how to dash full gallop into a forest of bristling spears, is no judge of that caution which is not less necessary than courage to the issue of a successful campaign. The coolest and most practical thinker of all antiquity, and at the same time the man of the widest range of accurate knowledge, Aristotle, whose name is almost a guarantee for right opinion in all things, laid it down as the most useful rule to guide men in the difficult art of living, that virtue or wise action lies in the mean between the two extremes of too little and too much. Those who are just starting in the career of life, however fond they may be of strong phrases, strong passions, unbridled energies, and exuberant demonstrations of all kinds, may rely on it, that as they grow in true manhood they will grow in all sorts of moderation, and learn to recognise the great truth that those are the strongest men, not who the most wantonly indulge, but who the most carefully curb their activities. What is called "seediness," after a debauch, is a plain proof that nature has been outraged, and will have her penalty. All debauch is incipient suicide; it is the unseen current beneath the house which sooner or later washes away the foundations. So it is with study. Long-continued intense mental exercise, especially in that ungrateful and ungenial form of the acquisition of knowledge called CRAM, weakens the brain, disorders the stomach, and makes the general action of the whole organism languid and unemphatic. Be warned, therefore, in time; violent methods will certainly produce violent results; and a vessel that once gets a crack, though it may be cunningly mended, will never stand such rough usage as a whole one. Wisdom is a good thing; but it is not good even to be wise always. "Be not wise overmuch: Why shouldst thou die before thy time?" Remember who said that.

X. If Great Britain be unquestionably the richest country in the world,—so much so indeed that Sydney Smith, always witty and always wise, felt himself justified in saying, that it is "the only country in which poverty is a crime," then certainly it is of paramount importance that every young man, when starting in the race of life in this country, should stamp into his soul the fundamental principle of all moral philosophy, that the real dignity of a man lies not in what he *has*, but in what he *is*. " The kingdom of heaven is within you,"—not without. Beware, therefore, of being infected by the moral contagion which more or less taints the atmosphere of every rich trading and manufacturing community, — the contagion which breeds a habit of estimating the value of men by the external apparatus of life rather than by its internal nobility. A dwarf, perched upon a lofty platform, looks over the heads of the multitude, and has no doubt this advantage from his position. So it is with the rich man who is merely rich; he acquires a certain social position, and from this, perhaps, gets M.P. tagged to his name; but, take the creature down from his artificial elevation, and look him fairly in the face, and you will find that he is a figure too insignificant to measure swords with. Fix this, therefore, in your minds, before all things, that there are few things in social life more contemptible than a rich man who stands upon his riches. By the very act of placing so high a value on the external, he has lapsed from the true character of his kind, and inverted the poles of human value. Have money,—by all means,—as much as to enable you to pay your tailor's bill, and, if possible, have a comfortable glass of claret or port to help you to digest your dinner; but never set your heart on what they call making a fortune. Socrates, Plato, Aristotle, and St. Paul (1 Tim. vi. 9), all agree in stating, with serious emphasis, that money-making is

not an ennobling occupation, and that he who
values money most values himself least. Stand
strictly on your moral and intellectual excellence, and you will find in the long run, when
the true value of things comes out, that there is
not a Duke or a millionaire in the land who can
boast himself your superior.

XI. I have no intention of running through
the catalogue of the virtues,—you must go to
Aristotle for that; but one grace of character,
which is an essential element of moral greatness,
and a sure pledge of all kinds of success, I cannot omit, and that is PERSEVERANCE. I never
knew a man good for anything in the world,
who, when he got a piece of work 'to do, did
not know how to stick to it. The poet Words-
worth, in his " Excursion," when the sky began
to look cloudy, gives, as a reason for going on
with his mountain perambulation, that though
a little rain might be disagreeable to the skin,
the act of giving up a fixed purpose, in view of
a slight possible inconvenience, is dangerous
to the character. There is much wisdom here.
We do not live in a world in which a man can
afford to be discouraged by trifles. There are real
difficulties enough, with which to fight is to
live, and which to conquer is to live nobly. A
friend of mine, making the ascent of Ben
Cruachan, when he had reached what he imagined to be the top, found that the real peak
was two miles farther on to the west, and that
the road to it lay along a rough stony ridge not
easy for weary feet to tread on. But this was

a small matter. The peak was being enveloped in mist, and it was only an hour from sunset. He wisely determined to take the nearest way down; but what did he do next day? He ascended the Ben again, and took his dinner triumphantly on the topmost top, in order, as he said, that the name of this most beautiful of Highland Bens might not for ever be associated in his mind with bafflement and defeat. This sort of a man, depend upon it, will succeed in everything he undertakes. Never boggle at a difficulty, especially at the commencement of a new work. *Aller Anfang ist schwer,*—all beginnings are difficult, as the German proverb says; and the more excellent the task the greater the difficulty. Χαλεπὰ τὰ καλά. Difficult things, in fact, are the only things worth doing, and they are done by a determined will and a strong hand. In the world of action will is power; persistent will, with circumstances not altogether unfavourable, is victory; nay, in the face of circumstances altogether unfavourable, persistency will carve out a way to unexpected success. Read the life of Frederick the Great of Prussia, and you will understand what this means. Fortune never will favour the man who flings away the dice-box because the first throw brings a low number.

I will now conclude with a few remarks on some of the best methods of acquiring moral excellence.

XII. The first thing to be attended to here

is to have it distinctly and explicitly graved into the soul, that there is only one thing that can give significance and dignity to human life—viz. VIRTUOUS ENERGY; and that this energy is attainable only by energising. If you imagine you are to be much helped by books, and reasons, and speculations, and learned disputations, in this matter, you are altogether mistaken. Books and discourses may indeed awaken and arouse you, and perhaps hold up the sign of a wise finger-post to prevent you from going astray at the first start, but they cannot move you a single step on the road; it is your own legs only that can perform the journey; it is altogether a matter of doing. Finger-posts are very well where you find them; but the sooner you can learn to do without them the better; for you will not travel long, depend upon it, before you come into regions of moor, and mist, and bog, and far waste solitudes; and woe be to the wayfarer, in such case, who has taught himself to travel only by finger-posts and mile-stones! You must have a compass of sure direction in your own soul, or you may be forced to depend for your salvation on some random saviour, who is only a little less bewildered than yourself. Gird up your loins, therefore, and prove the all-important truth, that as you learn to walk only by walking, to leap by leaping, and to fence by fencing, so you can learn to live nobly only by acting nobly on every occasion that presents itself. If you shirk the first trial of your manhood, you will come so much the weaker to the second; and if the next occasion, and the next again, finds you unprepared, you will infallibly sink into baseness. A swimmer becomes strong to stem the tide only by frequently breasting the big waves. If you practise always in shallow waters, your heart will assuredly fail you in the hour of high flood. General notions about sin and salvation can do you no good in the way of the blessed life. As in a journey, you must see milestone after milestone fall into your rear, otherwise you remain stationary; so, in the grand march of a noble life, one paltriness after another must disappear, or you have lost your chance.

XIII. Richter gives it as one excellent antidote against moral depression, to call up in our darkest moments the memory of our brightest; so, in the dusty struggle and often tainted atmosphere of daily business, it is well to carry about with us the purifying influence of a high ideal of human conduct, fervidly and powerfully expressed. Superstitious persons carry amulets externally on their breasts: carry you a select store of holy texts within, and you will be much more effectively armed against the powers of evil than any most absolute monarch behind a bristling body-guard. Such texts you may find occurring in many places, from the Kalidasas and Sakyamunis of the East, to Pythagoras, Plato, Aristotle, and Epictetus, in the West; but if you are wise, and above the seduction of showy and pretentious novelties, you will store your memory early in youth with the golden texts of the Old and New Testaments; and, as the Bible is a big book—not so much a book, indeed, as a great literature in small bulk,—perhaps I could not do better in this place than indicate for you a few books or chapters which you will find it of inestimable value to graft into your soul deeply before you come much into contact with those persons of coarse moral fibre, low aspirations, and lukewarm temperament, commonly called men of the world. First, of course, there is the Sermon on the Mount, then the 13th chapter of the 1st Epistle to the Corinthians; then the Gospel of John; then the General Epistle of James; the two Epistles to Timothy; the 8th chapter of the Romans; the 5th and 6th chapters of the Ephesians; and the same chapters of the Galatians. In the Old Testament every day's experience will reveal to you more clearly the profound wisdom of the Book of Proverbs. As a guide through life it is not possible to find a better directory than this book; and I remember the late Principal Lee, who knew Scotland well, saying with emphasis, that our country owed no small part of the practical sagacity for which it is so famed, to an early familiarity with this body of practical wisdom, which, in old times, used to be printed separately, and found in every man's pocket. For seasons of devout meditation, of course, the Psalms of the great minstrel monarch are more to be commended; and among them I should recommend specially, as calculated to infuse a spirit of deep and catholic piety into the souls of the young,—Psalms i. viii. xix. xxiv. xxxii. xxxvii. xlix. li. liii. lxxiii. xc. ciii.

civ. cvii. cxxi. cxxxi. cxxxiii. And these Psalms ought not only to be frequently read, till they make rich the blood of the soul with a genial and generous piety, but they ought to be sung to their proper music till they create round us a habitual atmosphere of pure and elevated sentiment, which we breathe as the breath of our higher life. This is the sort of emotional drill which that grand old heathen Plato enjoins with such eloquence in some of the wisest chapters of his lofty-minded polity, but a drill which we British Christians, with all our pretensions, in these latter times seem somewhat backward to understand.

XIV. Perhaps even more important towards the achievement of a noble life than a memory well stored with sacred texts, is an imagination well decorated with heroic pictures; in other words, there is no surer method of becoming good, and it may be great also, than an early familiarity with the lives of great and good men. So far as my experience goes, there is no kind of sermon so effective as the example of a great man. Here we see the thing done before us,—actually done,—a thing of which we were not even dreaming; and the voice speaks forth to us with a potency like the voice of many waters, "*Go thou and do likewise.*" Why not? No doubt, not every man is a hero; and heroic opportunities are not given every day; but if you cannot do the same thing, you may do something like it; if you are not planted on as high or as large a stage, you can show as much manhood, and manifest as much virtuous persistency, on a small scale. Every man may profit by the example of truly great men, if he is bent on making the most of himself and his circumstances. It is altogether a delusion to measure the greatness of men by the greatness of the stage on which they act, or the volume of the sound with which the world loves to reverberate their achievements. A Moltke in council, on the eve of a great battle which is to shift the centre of gravity of our western political system, is only acting on a maxim of practical wisdom that requires to be applied with as much discrimination, tact, and delicacy, by the provost of a provincial town planning a water-bill or a tax for the improvement of the city. Nay, that moral heroism is often greatest of which the world says least, and which is exercised in the humblest spheres, and in circles the most unnoticed. Let us therefore turn our youthful imaginations into great picture-galleries and Walhallas of the heroic souls of all times and all places; and we shall be incited to follow after good, and be ashamed to commit any sort of baseness in the direct view of such " a cloud of witnesses." Would you know what faith means, leave Calvinists and Arminians to split straws about points of doctrine; but do you read and digest that splendid eleventh chapter of the Hebrews, and you will escape for ever from the netted snares of theological logomachy. In this sublime chapter the great Apostle is merely giving a succinct summation of the method of teaching by concrete examples, with which the Scriptures are so richly studded, and of which our modern sermons are mostly so destitute. When I see our young men lolling on sofas, and grinning over those sorry caricatures of humanity with which the pages of Thackeray and other popular novelists are filled, I often wonder what sort of a human life can be expected to grow up from that early habit of learning to sneer, or at best, to be amused, at an age when seriousness and devout admiration are the only seeds out of which any future nobleness can be expected to grow. For myself, I honestly confess that I never could learn anything from Thackeray; there is a certain feeble amiability even about his best characters, which, if it is free from the depressing influence of his bad ones, is certainly anything but bracing. One of the best of Greek books, once in everybody's hands, now, I fear, fallen considerably into the shade, is Plutarch.* Here you have, whether for youth or manhood, in the shape of living examples of the most rich and various type, the very stuff from which human efficiency must ever be made. Our accurate critical historians have a small educational value when set against that fine instinct for all true human greatness, and that genial sympathy with all human weakness, which shine out so conspicuously in the classical picture-gallery of that rare old Bœotian. Let therefore our young men study to make themselves familiar, not with the fribbles, oddities,

* "I read with great delight Langhorne's translation of Plutarch."—J. S. Mill, *Autobiography.*

and monstrosities of humanity, set forth in fictitious narratives, but with the real blood and bone of human heroism which the select pages of biography present. An Athenian Pericles, with noble magnanimity, telling his servant to take a lamp and show a scurrilous reviler politely the way home; a German Luther, having his feet shod with the gospel of peace, and the sword of the Spirit in his hands, marching with cheerful confidence against an embattled array of kaisers and cardinals; a Pastor Oberlin in a remote mountain parish of Alsace, flinging behind him the bland allurements of metropolitan preferment, and turning his little rocky diocese into a moral and physical paradise,—these are great stereotyped FACTS, which should drive themselves like goads into the hearts of the young. No man can contradict a fact; but the best fictions, without a deep moral significance beneath, are only iridescent froth, beautiful now, but which a single puff of air blows into nothingness.

XV. Better, much better, than even the mirror of greatness in the biographies of truly great men, is the living influence of such men when you have the happiness of coming in contact with them. The best books are only a clever machinery for stirring the nobler nature. but they act indirectly and feebly; they may be remote also, dry and dusty upon the library shelves, not even on your table, and very far from your heart. But a living great man, coming across your path, carries with him an

electric influence which you cannot escape—
that is, of course if you are capable of being
affected in a noble way, for the blind do not
see, and the dead do not feel; and there is a
class of people—very reputable people perhaps
in their way—in whose breasts the epiphany
of a Christ will only excite the remark, "*He
hath a devil!*" Supposing, however, that
you are not one of the Scribes and Pharisees,
but a young man starting on the journey of
life with a reverential receptiveness and a
delicate sensibility, such as belong to well-
conditioned youth, in this case the greatest
blessing that can happen to you is to come
directly into contact with some truly great man,
and the closer the better; for it is only the
morally noble, and not the intellectually clever,
in whom greater intimacy always reveals greater
excellences. To have felt the thrill of a fervid
humanity shoot through your veins at the touch
of a Chalmers, a Macleod, or a Bunsen, is to a
young man of a fine susceptibility worth more
than all the wisdom of the Greeks, all the
learning of the Germans, and all the sagacity of
the Scotch. After such a vivific influence, the
light witlings may sneer as they please, and
the grave Gamaliels may frown; but you know
in whom you have believed, and you believe
because you have seen, and you grow with a
happy growth, and your veins are full of sap,
because you have been engrafted into the stem
of a true vine. And if it be not your good
fortune to come under the direct genial expan-
sive virtue of some great moral sun, you are not

altogether left to chance in the moral influences with which you are surrounded. If you cannot always avoid the contagion of low company, you may at all events ban yourself from voluntarily marching into it. There are few situations in life where you may not have some power of choosing your companions; and remember that moral contagion, like the infectious power of physical diseases, borrows half its strength from the weakness of the subject with which it comes in contact. If you were only half as pure as Christ, you might go about with harlots and be nothing the worse for it. As it is, however, and considering the weakness of the flesh, and the peculiar temptations of puberty, the best thing you can do is to make a sacred vow, on no occasion and on no account to keep company with persons who will lead you into haunts of dissipation and debauchery. No amount of hilarious excitement or momentary sensuous lustihood can compensate for the degradation which your moral nature must suffer by associating, on familiar and tolerant terms with the most degraded and abandoned of the human species. There can be no toleration for vice. We may, yea and we ought, to weep for the sinner, but we must not sport with the sin. Remember in this regard what happened to Robert Burns. He knew very well how to preach, but his practice was a most miserable performance, reminding us at every step of the terrible sarcastic sentence of Pliny, "*There is nothing more proud or more paltry than* MAN." Have you care that you do not follow the example of that mischanceful bard, without having his hot blood and high-pressure vitality to excuse or to palliate your follies. Let your company be always, where possible, better than yourself; and when you have the misfortune to move amongst your inferiors, bear in mind this seriously, that if you do not seize the apt occasion to draw them up to your level—which requires wisdom as well as love—they will certainly not be slow to drag you down to theirs.

XVI. "Men may try many things," said the wise old bard of Weimar; "only not live at random;" and if you would not live at random, it will be necessary for you to fix set times for calling yourself to account. In commercial transactions it is found a great safeguard against debt, to pay for everything, as much as possible, in cash, and, where that is not possible, not to run long accounts, but to strike clear balances at certain set seasons. Exactly so in our accounts with God and with our souls. The best charts and the most accurate compasses will bring no profit to the man who does not get into the habit of regularly using them. In this view the illustrious practice of the old Pythagoreans (who were a church as much as a school) presents a good model for us.

" Let not soft sleep usurp oblivious sway
  Till thrice you've told the deeds that mark'd the day :
  Whither thy steps ? what thing for thee most fitted
  Was aptly done ? and what good deed omitted ?
  And when you've summed the tale, wipe out the bad
  With gracious grief, and in the good be glad ! "

No man, in my opinion, will ever attain to high excellence in what an excellent old divine calls "the life of God in the soul of man," without cultivating stated periods of solitude, and using that solitude for the important purpose of self-knowledge and self-amelioration. "Commune with your own heart on your bed, and be still," said the Psalmist.

> "Who never ate with tears his bread,
>   And through the long-drawn midnight hours
> Sat weeping on his lonely bed,
>   He knows you not, ye heavenly Powers!"

are the well-known words of a poet who certainly cannot be accused of being either Methodistical in his habits or mawkish in his tone. "Let not the sun go down upon your wrath," said St. Paul;—all which utterances plainly imply the utility of such stated seasons of moral review as the Pythagorean verses prescribe, and as we see now in most European countries in the institution of the Christian Sabbath waiting to be utilised. No doubt the Jewish Sabbath was originally instituted simply for the rest of the body; and it was most wise and politic that this Christian's "Lord's-day," set apart for a purely religious purpose, should have adopted this hygienic element also into its composition; but with such a fair arena of enlargement opened periodically, bringing perfect freedom from the trammels of engrossing professions, he is not a wise man who does not devote at least one part of the Christian Sabbath to the serious work of moral self-review. Not a few severe

criticisms have been made by foreigners on
what has been called the "bitter observance" of
the Sunday by the Scotch; but these hasty
critics ought to have reflected how much of the
solidity, sobriety, and general reliability of the
Scottish character is owing to their serious and
thoughtful observance of these recurrent periods
of sacred rest. The eternal whirl and fiddle of
life, so characteristic of our gay Celtic neigh-
bours across the Channel, is apt to beget an
excitability and a frivolity in the conduct of
even the most serious affairs, which is incom-
patible with true moral greatness. If we Scotch
impart somewhat of an awful character to our
piety by not singing on Sunday, the French
certainly would march much more steadily, and
more creditably, on the second day of the week,
if they cultivated a more sober tone on the
first.

XVII. In connection with the delicate function of moral self-review, it occurs naturally to
mention PRAYER. In this scientific age, when
everything is analysed, and anatomised, and
tabulated, there is a tendency to talk of knowledge as a power to which all things are subject.
But the maxim that knowledge is power is true
only where knowledge is the main thing wanted.
There are higher things than knowledge in the
world; there are living energies; and in the
moral world, certainly, it is not knowledge but
aspiration that is the moving power, and the
wing of aspiration is prayer. Where aspiration
is wanting, the soul creeps; it cannot fly; it

is at best a caged bird, curiously busy in counting and classifying the bars of its own confinement. Of course, we do not mean that any person should be so full of his own little self, and so ignorant of the grandeur of the universe, as to besiege the ear of Heaven with petitions that the laws of the universe shall be changed any moment that may suit his convenience. We do not pray that we may alter the Divine decrees, but that our human will may learn to move in harmony with the Divine will. How far with regard to any special matter, not irrevocably fixed in the Divine concatenation of possibilities, our petition may prevail, we never can tell; but this we do know, that the most natural and the most effectual means of keeping our own noblest nature in harmony with the source of all vital nobleness, is to hold high emotional communion with that source, and to plant ourselves humbly in that attitude of devout receptiveness which is the one becoming attitude in the created towards the Creator. Practically, there is no surer test of a man's moral diathesis than the capacity of prayer. He, at least in a Christian country, must be an extremely ignorant man, who could invoke the Divine blessing day after day on acts of manifest turpitude, falsehood. or folly. In the old heathen times, a man in certain circumstances might perhaps, with a clear conscience, have prayed to a Dionysius or an Aphrodite to consecrate his acts of drunkenness or debauchery; but, thanks to the preaching of the Galilean fishermen, we have got beyond that now; and universal experience declares the fact that genuine private prayer (for I do not speak of course of repeating routine formularies), which is the vital element of a noble moral nature, is to the coarse, sensual, and selfish man, an atmosphere which he cannot breathe. Take, therefore, young man, the apostolic maxim with you —PRAY WITHOUT CEASING. Keep yourself always in an attitude of reverential dependence on the Supreme Source of all good. It is the most natural and speediest and surest antidote against that spirit of shallow self-confidence and brisk impertinence so apt to spring up with the knowledge without charity which puffeth up and edifieth not. What a pious tradition has taught us to do daily before our principal meal, as a comely ceremony, let us learn to do before every serious act of our life, not as a cold form, but as a fervid reality. Go forth to battle, brave young man, like David, with your stone ready, and your sling well poised; but be sure that you are fighting the battle of the God of Israel, not of the devil. Whether you have a sword or a pen in your hand, wield neither the one nor the other in a spirit of insolent self-reliance or of vain self-exhibition; and, not less in the hour of exuberant enjoyment than in the day of dark despondency and despair, be always ready to say,—" BLESS ME, EVEN ME ALSO, O MY FATHER!"

THE END.

BOOKS PUBLISHED BY

DAVID DOUGLAS

10 CASTLE STREET,
EDINBURGH, *March* 1890.

AMERICAN AUTHORS.

AMERICAN AUTHORS.

Latest Editions. Revised by the Authors. In 1s. volumes.
By Post, 1s. 2d.

Printed by Constable, and published with the sanction of the Authors.

By W. D. HOWELLS.
A Foregone Conclusion.
A Chance Acquaintance.
Their Wedding Journey.
A Counterfeit Presentment.
The Lady of the Aroostook. 2 vols.
Out of the Question.
The Undiscovered Country. 2 vols.
A Fearful Responsibility.
Venetian Life. 2 vols.
Italian Journeys. 2 vols.
The Rise of Silas Lapham. 2 vols.
Indian Summer. 2 vols.

By FRANK R. STOCKTON.
Rudder Grange.
The Lady or the Tiger?
A Borrowed Month.

By GEORGE W. CURTIS.
Prue and I.

By J. C. HARRIS (*Uncle Remus*).
Mingo, and other Sketches.

By GEO. W. CABLE.
Old Creole Days.
Madame Delphine.

By B. W. HOWARD.
One Summer.

By MARY E. WILKINS.
A Humble Romance.
A Far-away Melody.

By JOHN BURROUGHS.
Winter Sunshine.
Pepacton.
Locusts and Wild Honey.
Wake-Robin.
Birds and Poets.
Fresh Fields.

By OLIVER WENDELL HOLMES.
The Autocrat of the Breakfast Table. 2 vols.
The Poet. 2 vols.
The Professor. 2 vols.

By G. P. LATHROP.
An Echo of Passion.

By R. G. WHITE.
Mr. Washington Adams.

By T. B. ALDRICH.
The Queen of Sheba.
Marjorie Daw.
Prudence Palfrey.
The Stillwater Tragedy. 2 vols.
Wyndham Towers: A Poem.

By B. MATTHEWS and H. C. BUNNER.
In Partnership.

By WILLIAM WINTER.
Shakespeare's England.
Wanderers: A Collection of Poems.

⁎ *Other Volumes of this attractive Series in preparation.*

Any of the above may be had bound in Cloth extra, at 2s. each volume.

'A set of charming little books.'—*Blackwood's Magazine.*
'A remarkably pretty series.'—*Saturday Review.*
'These neat and minute volumes are creditable alike to printer and publisher.'—*Pall Mall Gazette.*
'The most graceful and delicious little volumes with which we are acquainted.'—*Freeman.*
'Soundly and tastefully bound . . . a little model of typography, . . . and the contents are worthy of the dress.'—*St. James's Gazette.*
'The delightful shilling series of "American Authors" introduced by Mr. David Douglas, has afforded pleasure to thousands of persons.'—*Figaro.*
'The type is delightfully legible, and the page is pleasant for the eye to rest upon; even in these days of cheap editions we have seen nothing that has pleased us so well.'—*Literary World.*

EDINBURGH: DAVID DOUGLAS.

SCOTTISH STORIES AND SKETCHES.

Johnny Gibb of Gushetneuk in the Parish of Pyketillim,
with Glimpses of Parish Politics about A.D. 1843, by WILLIAM ALEXANDER LL.D. Ninth Edition, with Glossary, Fcap. 8vo, 2s.

Seventh Edition, with Twenty Illustrations—Portraits and Landscapes—by GEORGE REID, R.S.A. Demy 8vo, 12s. 6d.

'A most vigorous and truthful delineation of local character, drawn from a portion of the country where that character is peculiarly worthy of careful study and record.'—*The Right Hon. W. E. Gladstone.*

'It is a grand addition to our pure Scottish dialect; . . . it is not merely a capital specimen of genuine Scottish northern *dialect;* but it is a capital specimen of pawky characteristic Scottish humour. It is full of good hard Scottish dry fun.'—*Dean Ramsay.*

Life among my Ain Folk, by the Author of 'JOHNNY GIBB OF GUSHETNEUK.'

Contents.

1. Mary Malcolmson's Wee Maggie.
2. Couper Sandy.
3. Francie Herriegerie's Sharger Laddie.
4. Baubie Huie's Bastard Geet.
5. Glengillodram.

Fcap. 8vo. Second Edition. Cloth, 2s. 6d. Paper, 2s.

'Mr. Alexander thoroughly understands the position of men and women who are too often treated with neglect, and graphically depicts their virtues and vices, and shows to his readers difficulties, struggles, and needs which they are sure to be the wiser for taking into view.'—*Freeman.*

Notes and Sketches of Northern Rural Life in the Eighteenth Century, by the Author of 'JOHNNY GIBB OF GUSHETNEUK.' In 1 vol. Fcap. 8vo, 2s. and 1s.

'This delightful little volume. It is a treasure. . . . We admire the telling simplicity of the style, the sly, pawky, Aberdonian humour, the wide acquaintance with the social and other conditions of the northern rural counties of last century, and the fund of illustrative anecdotes which enrich the volume. The author has done great service to the cause of history and of progress. It is worth a great many folios of the old dry-as-dust type.'—*Daily Review.*

Chronicles of Glenbuckie, by HENRY JOHNSTON, Author of 'The Dawsons of Glenara.' Extra Fcap. 8vo. 5s.

⁎⁎* A book of humour and pathos, descriptive of the social, political, and ecclesiastical life in a Scottish parish of fifty years ago.

'A genuine bit of Scottish literature.'—*Scottish Leader.*

Scotch Folk. Illustrated. Third Edition enlarged. Fcap. 8vo, price 1s.

'They are stories of the best type, quite equal in the main to the average of Dean Ramsay's well-known collection.'—*Aberdeen Free Press.*

Rosetty Ends, or the Chronicles of a Country Cobbler.
By Job Bradawl (A. DEWAR WILLOCK), Author of 'She Noddit to me.' Fcap. 8vo, Illustrated. 2s. and 1s.

'The sketches are amusing productions, narrating comical incidents, connected by a thread of common character running through them all—a thread waxed into occasional strength by the 'roset' of a homely, entertaining wit.'—*Scotsman.*

EDINBURGH: DAVID DOUGLAS.

LITTLE BROWN BOOKS.

Foolscap 8vo, Sixpence each.

The Religion of Humanity: An Address delivered at the Church Congress, Manchester, October 1888, by the Right Hon. ARTHUR J. BALFOUR, M.P., LL.D., etc., 6d.

'We have called the pamphlet a sermon because it is one, though the fitting text, "The fool hath said in his heart, There is no God," is courteously omitted; and we venture to say that of all who will read it, not one per cent. ever read or heard one more convincing or intellectually more delightful.'—*Spectator.*

[*A large type edition of this may also be had in cloth at 5s.*]

Fishin' Jimmy, by A. T. SLOSSON. 6d. '*A choice story from America.*'

'A story from which, in its simplicity and pathos, we may all learn lessons of wisdom and charity.'—*Freeman.*

'A pathetic but pretty little story, telling the simple life of one possessed of a profound veneration for all things heavenly, yet viewing them with the fearless questioning eyes of the child.'—*Literary World.*

'Macs' in Galloway. By PATRICK DUDGEON. 6d.

Rab and his Friends. By Dr. JOHN BROWN. 6d.

Marjorie Fleming. By Dr. JOHN BROWN. 6d.

Our Dogs. By Dr. JOHN BROWN. 6d.

'With Brains, Sir.' By Dr. JOHN BROWN. 6d.

Minchmoor. By Dr. JOHN BROWN. 6d.

Jeems the Door-Keeper. By Dr. JOHN BROWN. 6d.

The Enterkin. By Dr. JOHN BROWN. 6d.

Plain Words on Health. By Dr. JOHN BROWN. 6d.

Something about a Well: with more of Our Dogs. By Dr. JOHN BROWN. 6d.

WORKS BY DR. JOHN BROWN.

Horæ Subsecivæ. 3 Vols. 22s. 6d.

Vol. I. Locke and Sydenham. Fifth Edition, with Portrait by James Faed. Crown 8vo, 7s. 6d.

Vol. II. Rab and his Friends. Thirteenth Edition. Crown 8vo, 7s. 6d.

Vol. III. John Leech. Fifth Edition, with Portrait by George Reid, R.S.A. Crown 8vo, 7s. 6d.

Rab and his Friends. With India-proof Portrait of the Author after Faed, and seven Illustrations after Sir G. Harvey, Sir Noel Paton, Mrs. Blackburn, and G. Reid, R.S.A. Demy 4to, cloth, 9s.

Marjorie Fleming: A Sketch. Being a Paper entitled 'Pet Marjorie; A Story of a Child's Life fifty years ago.' New Edition, with Illustrations by Warwick Brookes. Demy 4to, 7s. 6d. and 6s.

Rab and his Friends. Cheap Illustrated Edition. Square 12mo ornamental wrapper, 1s.

EDINBURGH: DAVID DOUGLAS.

SCRIPTURE HISTORY, ETC.

Rev. John Ker, D.D.
SERMONS: FIRST SERIES. 14th Edition. Crown 8vo, . . . 6s. 0d.
SERMONS: SECOND SERIES. Fifth Thousand. Crown 8vo, . . 6s. 0d.
THOUGHTS FOR HEART AND LIFE. Ex. Fcap. 8vo, . . . 4s. 6d.
LETTERS: 1866-1885. Crown 8vo, ... 4s. 6d.

Rev. George Bowen, of Bombay.
DAILY MEDITATIONS. New Edition. Sm. 4to, ... 5s. 0d.
LOVE REVEALED. New Edition. Sm. 4to, ... 5s. 0d.
THE AMENS OF CHRIST. Sm. 4to, ... 5s. 0d.

Thomas Erskine, of Linlathen.
THE LETTERS OF. Edited by Dr. HANNA. New Edition. Cr. 8vo, . 7s. 6d.
THE UNCONDITIONAL FREENESS OF THE GOSPEL. Cr. 8vo, . . 3s. 6d.
THE BRAZEN SERPENT, OR LIFE COMING THROUGH DEATH. Cr. 8vo, 5s. 0d.
THE INTERNAL EVIDENCE OF REVEALED RELIGION. Cr. 8vo, . 5s. 0d.
THE SPIRITUAL ORDER. Cr. 8vo, ... 5s. 0d.
THE DOCTRINE OF ELECTION. Cr. 8vo, ... 6s. 0d.
THE FATHERHOOD OF GOD. Ex. Fcap. 8vo, ... 1s. 0d.

William Hanna, D.D., LL.D.
THE EARLIER YEARS OF OUR LORD. Ex. Fcap. 8vo, . . . 5s. 0d.
THE MINISTRY IN GALILEE. Ex. Fcap. 8vo, ... 5s. 0d.
THE CLOSE OF THE MINISTRY. Ex. Fcap. 8vo, ... 5s. 0d.
THE PASSION WEEK. Ex. Fcap. 8vo, ... 5s. 0d.
THE LAST DAY OF OUR LORD'S PASSION. Ex. Fcap. 8vo, . . 5s. 0d.
THE FORTY DAYS AFTER THE RESURRECTION. Ex. Fcap. 8vo, . 5s. 0d.
THE RESURRECTION OF THE DEAD. Ex. Fcap. 8vo, . . . 5s. 0d.
MEMOIRS OF THE REV. THOS. CHALMERS. 2 vols. Cr. 8vo, . 12s. 0d.

William F. Skene, D.C.L.
THE GOSPEL HISTORY FOR THE YOUNG. 3 vols. Sm. Cr. 8vo, . 7s. 6d.

Rev. Walter C. Smith, D.D.
THE SERMON ON THE MOUNT. Cr. 8vo, ... 6s. 0d.

Professor Blackie.
ON SELF-CULTURE. Fcap. 8vo, ... 2s. 6d.

Principal Shairp.
STUDIES IN POETRY AND PHILOSOPHY. Cr. 8vo, ... 7s. 6d.
SKETCHES IN HISTORY AND POETRY. Cr. 8vo, ... 7s. 6d.
CULTURE AND RELIGION. Fcap. 8vo, ... 3s. 6d.

Professor Hodgson.
ERRORS IN THE USE OF ENGLISH. Cr. 8vo, ... 3s. 6d.

Mrs. M. M. Gordon.
WORK; OR, PLENTY TO DO AND HOW TO DO IT. Fcap. 8vo, . 2s. 6d.

Rev. Archibald Scott, D.D.
BUDDHISM AND CHRISTIANITY. Demy 8vo, ... 7s. 6d.

The Duke of Argyll.
WHAT IS TRUTH? Fcap. 8vo, ... 1s. 0d.

EDINBURGH: DAVID DOUGLAS.

SCOTTISH HISTORY AND ARCHAEOLOGY.

Celtic Scotland: A History of Ancient Alban. By WILLIAM F. SKENE, D.C.L., Historiographer-Royal for Scotland. In 3 vols. I. History and Ethnology. II. Church and Culture. III. Land and People. Demy 8vo, 45s. Illustrated with Maps.

Scotland under her Early Kings. A History of the Kingdom to the close of the 13th century. By E. WILLIAM ROBERTSON. In 2 vols. 8vo, cloth, 36s.

The History of Liddesdale, Eskdale, Ewesdale, Wauchopedale, and the Debateable Land. Part I., from the Twelfth Century to 1530. By ROBERT BRUCE ARMSTRONG. The edition is limited to 275 copies demy quarto, and 105 copies on large paper (10 inches by 13), 42s. and 84s.

View of the Political State of Scotland in the last Century. A Confidential Report on the Political Opinions, Family Connections, or Personal Circumstances, of the 2662 County Voters in 1788. Edited, with an introductory account of the Law relating to County Elections, by Sir CHARLES ELPHINSTONE ADAM of Blair-Adam, Bart., Barrister-at-Law. Crown 8vo, 5s.

The Castellated and Domestic Architecture of Scotland, from the Twelfth to the Eighteenth Century. By DAVID M'GIBBON and THOMAS ROSS, Architects. 4 vols., with about 2000 Illustrations of Ground Plans, Sections, Views, Elevations, and Details. Royal 8vo. 42s. each vol. Net.

Scotland in Early Christian Times. By JOSEPH ANDERSON, LL.D., Keeper of the National Museum of the Antiquaries of Scotland. (Being the Rhind Lectures in Archæology for 1879 and 1880.) 2 vols. Demy 8vo, profusely Illustrated. 12s. each volume.

Scotland in Pagan Times. By JOSEPH ANDERSON, LL.D. (Being the Rhind Lectures in Archæology for 1881 and 1882.) In 2 vols. Demy 8vo, profusely Illustrated. 12s. each volume.

The Past in the Present—What is Civilisation? (Being the Rhind Lectures in Archæology, delivered in 1876 and 1878.) By Sir ARTHUR MITCHELL, K.C.B., M.D., LL.D. Demy 8vo, with 148 Woodcuts, 15s.

Scotland as it was and as it is: A History of Races, Military Events, and the rise of Commerce. By the DUKE OF ARGYLL. Demy 8vo, illustrated, 7s. 6d.

Major Fraser's Manuscript. His Adventures in Scotland and England; his Mission to and Travels in France; his Services in the Rebellion (and his Quarrels) with Simon Fraser, Lord Lovat, 1696-1737. Edited by ALEXANDER FERGUSSON, Lieutenant-Colonel. 2 vols. fcap. 8vo, 12s.

Ecclesiological Notes on some of the Islands of Scotland, with other Papers relating to Ecclesiological Remains on the Scottish Mainland and Islands. By THOMAS S. MUIR, Author of 'Characteristics of Old Church Architecture,' etc. Demy 8vo, with numerous Illustrations, 21s.

The Hill Forts, Stone Circles, and other Structural Remains of Ancient Scotland. By C. MACLAGAN, Lady Associate of the Society of Antiquaries of Scotland. With Plans and Illustrations. Folio, 31s. 6d.

EDINBURGH: DAVID DOUGLAS.

OPEN-AIR BOOKS.

How to Catch Trout. By THREE ANGLERS. Illustrated, 1s. & 2s.

'The aim of this book is to give, within the smallest space possible, such practical information and advice as will enable the beginner, without further instruction, to attain moderate proficiency in the use of every legitimate lure.'

'A delightful little book, and one of great value to Anglers.'—*Scotsman*.

'The advice given is always sound.'—*Field*.

'The most practical and instructive work of its kind in the literature of angling.'—*Dundee Advertiser*.

'A well-written and thoroughly practical little book.'—*Land and Water*.

On Horse-breaking. By ROBERT MORETON. Second Edition, 1s.

A Year in the Fields. By JOHN WATSON. Fcap. 8vo, 1s.

'A charming little work. A lover of life in the open air will read the book with unqualified pleasure.'—*Scotsman*.

May in Anjou, with other Sketches and Studies. By ELEANOR C. PRICE, Author of 'A Lost Battle,' etc. Fcap. 8vo, 1s.

Iona. With Illustrations. By the DUKE OF ARGYLL. Fcap. 8vo, 1s.

Studies of Great Cities—Paris. By D. BALSILLIE, M.A. Fcap. 8vo, 1s.

On the Links; being Golfing Studies by various hands, with Shakespeare on Golf. By a NOVICE. Also two Rhymes on Golf by ANDREW LANG. Fcap. 8vo, 1s.

The Gamekeeper's Manual; being an Epitome of the Game Laws of England and Scotland, and of the Gun Licences and Wild Birds Acts. By ALEXANDER PORTER, Chief Constable of Roxburghshire. Second edition, crown 8vo, 3s.

'A concise and valuable epitome to the Game Laws, specially addressed to those engaged in protecting game.'—*Scotsman*.

'An excellent and compactly written little handbook.'—*Free Press*, Aberdeen.

The Art of Golf. By Sir W. G. SIMPSON, Bart. In 1 vol. demy 8vo, with twenty plates from instantaneous photographs of Professional Players, chiefly by A. F. Macfie, Esq. Price 15s.

'He has devoted himself for years with exemplary zeal to the collecting of everything which a true golfer would like to know about the royal game, and the result of his labour is worthy of the highest commendation. . . . The prominent feature of the volume is the set of illustrations. For the first time, by means of instantaneous photography, are produced on paper the movements made by players, with a classical style in the process of striking a golf ball.'—*Scotsman*.

Modern Horsemanship: A New Method of Teaching Riding and Training by means of Instantaneous Photographs from the Life. By E. L. ANDERSON. New Edition, re-written and re-arranged. In 1 vol. demy 8vo. Illustrated. Price 21s.

'The best new English work on riding and training that we can recommend is the book "Modern Horsemanship."'—*The Sport Zeitung*, Vienna.

'Every page shows the author to be a complete master of his subject.'—*The Field*.

How to know Grasses by the leaves. By A. N. M'ALPINE, B.Sc., with a Preface by Robert Wallace, F.R.S., etc., Professor of Agriculture, Edinburgh. Illustrated. 3s. 6d. net.

EDINBURGH: DAVID DOUGLAS.

www.ingramcontent.com/pod-product-compliance
Lightning Source LLC
Chambersburg PA
CBHW020151170426
43199CB00010B/990